PURPOSE IN THE PAIN

PURPOSE IN THE PAIN

Freshun E. Wilson

XULON PRESS

Xulon Press
2301 Lucien Way #415
Maitland, FL 32751
407.339.4217
www.xulonpress.com

Cover Design by: Sean Marcus Fowler
Photgraphs by: Michael Taylor Photography

Paperback ISBN-13: 978-1-66286-635-7
Hard Cover ISBN-13: 978-1-66286-636-4
Ebook ISBN-13: 978-1-66286-637-1

TABLE OF CONTENTS

Dedications ix
Introduction xi
Chapter 1: What IS Pain? 1
Chapter 2: TRUST is a MUST 9
Chapter 3: Rejoice In The Pain 15
Chapter 4: The Pain Of Divorce 23
Chapter 5: The Pain Of Betrayal 45
Chapter 6: Pain Of A Devastating Diagnosis 51
Chapter 7: Pain Gives Clarity 57
Chapter 8: Pain Equips Us To Help Others 63
Chapter 9: Pain Of Losing Loved Ones 69
Chapter 10: Pain Strengthens Our Dependence On God 79
Chapter 11: Healing From The Pain 83
Chapter 12: Love "You" After The Pain 89
Chapter 13: After The Pain 95
Chapter 14: Benefits Of Pain 99
Conclusion 105
About the Author 115

"PURPOSE IN THE PAIN"

DEDICATIONS

This book is dedicated to God, without whom I would have no story to share.

To my late parents Rev. Fredrick E. Wilson Sr. and Lady Anita L. Wilson. I am the woman I am today because of traits, talents and personalities that came directly from them. Even in physical absence, I feel their love and strength with me daily. I look forward to the day when we meet again.

To the loves of my life, my children H. Levi IV, Christopher, and Jazmyn. When I look at you, I know without a doubt I've done something right. I Love you kids.

To my brother and sister Fredrick Jr. and Anita M., the best siblings anyone could ever ask for. Thank you for your love and support. I love you.

INTRODUCTION

Have you ever stopped, taken a long look around and asked yourself the question, "How did I get here?" Have personal circumstances ever caused you to feel as though your life has been turned upside down? Have you ever felt as though struggle, hardship and pain invaded your life only to set up a permanent residence? Have disappointments in life ever caused you to question your purpose? Or have you ever found yourself overwhelmed with life to the point of simply wanting to give up? It could be the loss of a job or a marriage that has taken a turn for the worse. Maybe you've been given a poor doctor's report, or you're coping with the loss of a dear loved one. There may even be someone who is feeling that where you are in life right now is the end of your story. Whatever your source of pain or hardship may be, I've written to enlighten you of the fact that you're not alone and that your life is not over. Remember, since you are still alive, you STILL have hope and a purpose.

We all have a purpose in life. God saw to that when He created us. Not only did He see to it, but He also placed the potential in each of us to fulfill that purpose. It is not always easy to see or understand what that purpose is because purpose is not always visible. However, our problems are always very visible to us, so much so that it is sometimes difficult to understand the meaning in it all. My friend, experiencing pain in this life is inevitable and seems to come easy with little to no effort. This seems especially true when you find yourself experiencing one trial after the other. Thus, bringing the question to mind, "Lord, why am I experiencing so much pain?" As you begin to examine your life you may begin to wonder what you have done to cause yourself so much pain. But if you are not careful you can find yourself sinking into a pit of despair as you search for reasons to your ongoing suffering. This universal painful dose of reality has left many from all walks of life feeling wounded, weary, and defeated as though they have no hope. And sadly, many have chosen to drown in this continuous reality of pain and hardship not realizing that if not addressed with a proper perspective, it will only lead to a lifetime of misery.

You see my friend; God's plans for His children have never been for us to live a life of misery. Neither is His will for us to settle into a victim's mentality while going through the trials of life. Yes, your situation may feel unbearable right now, but recognize that you are not alone in your struggles. No matter how difficult the circumstances, we must not allow ourselves to get stuck in the circumstances as though we have no hope. What must be remembered is that God is with us during our times of pain, struggle, and hardship. We may not always feel Him or see Him, but never forget He is there with us. Oftentimes fear, doubt, frustration, depression, and other emotional or mental struggles, may cause some to give up and settle in their pain, thus denying themselves the amazing destiny which God has designed for their lives. But don't worry my friend, if you can relate, then this book was written to encourage you! Although it may seem impossible to keep going now, don't give up! As you continue walking, keep in mind that there is a GOOD PURPOSE in all of your suffering.

Before going any further, please allow me to ease your mind a bit by letting you know that you are not alone. By no means am I making light of your struggle and pain. Trust me when I say, I understand how real the struggle of experiencing pain in this life can truly be my friend. I know it doesn't feel good. I'm also aware of how difficult it is to see anything good coming from the pain when you're in the thick of it. I too have had times in my life when I've shared some of these exact sentiments. There have been times in my life when I wanted to give up. I've had times when it seemed as though the struggles and tears would never end. There have been times in my life when the pain I was experiencing felt unbearable at that moment. I've experienced fearful times that arrested me causing things to APPEAR that living in misery was best.

There is an old saying, "What comes from the heart reaches the heart." In all my reading, I've found that the best and most helpful books are those that have been written simply, truthfully, and straight from the heart. My friend, this book was shaped not by fiction, but instead by some of my own experiences in life. I've chosen to share pieces of my heart with you in hopes that you are strengthened and encouraged to truly TRUST in God despite any curveball's life may throw your way. Life is a journey for us all and none of us have all the answers to questions that may arise along the way. We will have many experiences on our journeys, some good and some bad. Some experiences will bring us joyful smiles, and others will bring us tears of sadness. The important thing to remember is that God is with us through them all. Oftentimes we may find ourselves tending to embrace the good times and dreading the painful times in life. But I've learned that if perceived correctly, both the joyful and painful experiences in life can be embraced recognizing that it all works together in making us who we are. The pain we experience in life is never wasted my friend. Always remember, there's a purpose in your pain! And no matter what the pain may be or where it stems from, stay mindful of the fact that God works all things together for our Good!

Chapter 1

WHAT IS PAIN?

As I stated before, experiencing pain and adversity in this life is inevitable. It must be understood that life doesn't always turn out the way we plan or expect it. There may be times in life when we're thrown for a loop, but what must be remembered even during those times is that our loving Father is there strengthening and carrying us through those times. My friend, I know firsthand how it feels to begin your marital journeys with joy and anticipation of starting a life filled with promise, but to end up with that joy coming to a screeching halt instead. I don't think anyone with good sense gets married to get divorced, at least I didn't. Life just seems to happen, and we do our best to walk through the tough times with God's help. I do however feel that sometimes couples may enter marriage without thinking clearly and considering some important things that truly matter when choosing a lifetime partner. But we'll get into that a little later.

I will say that the death of my marriage is one of the most painful experiences I've endured in my lifetime. However, the single most painful experience is losing my mother and my father.

Although I had been aware of the reality of death and had consoled many who've experienced death in their lives, being personally acquainted with death was something totally different. In the back of my mind, I knew that my parents wouldn't live forever, however losing them when I did was not how I saw it happening. Losing them both only two years apart, those were painful experiences that still hurt today. I understand how these, and other situations will numb you and arrest you to the point of saying, "I'll never be happy again."

Although our situations may not be identical, the point being made is that PAIN is PAIN and Pain hurts. Disappointments are inevitable. In this life you will experience some disappointments and shed some tears. Experiencing pain and suffering is not easy for anyone and yet it's something we will all have to endure at some point in life. You might be suffering with chronic pain, mental illness, cancer, kidney failure, financial hardship, broken relationships, a disability, or struggling with sin. There may be someone reading who's struggling with memories from mental or sexual abuse.

Betrayal may have even come knocking on your door unexpectedly as it did mine. I've found that the most hurtful thing about betrayal is that it never comes from your enemies. Think about that if you will. Experiences with betrayal can only come from someone close to you such as family or so-called friends. This is what causes betrayal to be so painful. It's painful because it comes from someone you've trusted in; someone you've spent quality time with. Betrayal comes from people we thought we knew. When you've been betrayed, your trust is negatively affected. You may find yourself looking around not knowing who in your circle is trustworthy or not. Experiencing betrayal causes one to begin questioning everything and everybody. And if not careful, this could lead to extreme paranoia. If your trust has ever been broken, then you my friend, have also felt the horrible sting of betrayal.

Being betrayed feels like a huge punch in the gut resulting in the very wind being knocked from your body. Betrayal causes major damage by breaking intimacy and security in relationships. This pain can cause very deep wounds and mental exhaustion. This type of pain causes emotional trauma. You see, when you experience betrayal, what you thought was true about a person turns out to be what's called a false positive. My experiences with betrayal and deception ALMOST caused me to lose my mind. However, although deeply wounded, I'm thankful to be standing on the other side of that pain today. My friend, I will continue to reiterate that pain is something we will all experience before leaving this earth.

Adversity will come. Negative situations will arise. It's been said that in life we're in one of three places, we're either in a storm, heading into a storm, or coming out of a storm. The point being made in that statement is that storms will come. No matter how much effort we may place in trying to avoid pain, storms, or suffering, in one way or another, they will all find a way into all of our lives. We can't run from it and shouldn't ignore it. Attempting to ignore pain will only delay your process of getting through it and healing properly. You may even be experiencing pain from some mistakes you've made in life.

No matter what the circumstances may be, three important things to remember are, you're not alone in your pain, you can overcome your pain and there is a purpose in your pain. You see my friend, God is with us and He uses our pain and suffering to reveal to us our ultimate dependence on Him and our hope in Him! We must understand that God's plans for us far exceed our circumstances. No matter how difficult, we can't allow ourselves to get stuck in our pain, mistakes, or circumstances. Remember that God can turn our mistakes into miracles! Therefore, instead of blaming yourself, blaming others or blaming God, whatever your painful circumstances may be, the proper response is," **God what are you saying to me through this situation?"**

Keep in mind that God never misses an opportunity to teach us. He knows us and what we need in order to better shape and conform us into His likeness. We must remember that God never promised us that we wouldn't have trouble. He never promised us He'd remove the trouble, but He DID promise to be with us IN the trouble. ***Psalm 46:1(KJV) lets us know that "God is our refuge and strength, a VERY present help in times of trouble"!*** As we hold on to this promise it will ease the fear of going through the trouble alone. The only way around suffering is to go THROUGH it. God wants us to know that real character is developed best not by evading pain, problems, and heartache, but by learning to endure them and to persevere until He has finished what He set out to do in our lives.

At one time in my life, I'd considered the pain of childbirth as the worst pain one could ever endure. You see, I'd endured 22 hours of labor with my first child which ended up with me having to have an emergency cesarean section. Although painful, I must admit that when I held my babies for the first time, it was worth all the pain I'd endured. Childbirth is an extremely painful and yet rewarding experience. There's no greater Joy than to give birth to your child. The nine months of carrying another little person in your body as he or she grows, flips, and kicks, watching yourself expand in all sorts of ways, and endure the hormonal changes that go along with it, all seems to go out the door when you finally see and hold the reward, your BABY!

The months of pain and struggle endured while carrying your baby is no longer the focus when holding your baby for the first time. I've undergone three Cesarean sections in giving birth to my children. And although a Cesarean section isn't considered a "natural process," it still has its pain you must endure before the healing process begins. After each surgery, the nurse explained to me how moving around would speed up my healing process. They encouraged me to move around through the pain instead of lying in bed. The nurse explained that walking around would increase blood flow and speed up the wound healing. They also explained that the failure to walk could increase weakness and put me at higher risks for other health problems. The way I was feeling at the time I thought she was crazy in telling me that. As much pain as I was experiencing there was no way that moving around would make it better. But, on the contrary it did. I decided to take her advice and try it and sure enough it worked! The more I walked through the pain the stronger my body felt. Complete healing took a little time but holding my beautiful bundles of Joy in the meantime made the process worthwhile!

Eventually I bounced back and was completely healed. If I would not have worked through it, the healing process could have taken much longer or not happened at all. I've found that the same applies to our dealing with pain in life. Life can throw us some heavy blows. Some things can happen in our lives that will completely turn our worlds upside down. Some will experience pain that pierces the heart and pain that feels impossible to bounce back from.

But remember this, the pain we will all suffer in life will leave us two choices. Those choices are to either stay there, dwindle, and die emotionally, mentally, spiritually, and physically, or we can choose to do what's necessary to get to the other side of the pain by allowing the pain to promote us to purpose.

What choice will you make? If you really want to get to the other side of your pain, my suggestion to you is that you work through your process. We ALL have a process. Although everyone's process may be different, what remains the same through them all is that God is willing and able to help us through "the process". And not only that, but He will also cause something good to come from it!

> Remember my friend, no matter what we go through in life, God will always go through it with us! In some cases, He'll hold our hands and walk with us and in other cases he may carry us. Whatever the case may be, the thing to remember is that GOD is always with us!

Pain is something that can affect you physically, mentally, spiritually, and emotionally, but the good thing is it won't kill you! As the saying goes, what doesn't kill you makes you stronger! Pain might shake you. It might temporarily arrest you. It might even cause you to press pause or reset, but it won't kill you. One thing pain will do is strengthen you if you will allow it to. Pain can propel you into your purpose. But you must be willing to trust God and go THROUGH the process. We do this by faith believing that God is there with us. And how do we know He's with us? We know it because His word tells us so. God Himself says in ***Hebrews 13:5 (NIV), "Never will I leave you; never will I forsake you."***

And as a believer I choose to stand on those words and my prayer is that you would do the same. YES, you CAN do it! I've found that the key to getting through times of difficulty is to first determine in your mind that you will NOT allow the PAIN in your life to forfeit your destiny. There will be times in life we will have to encourage ourselves just as King David did. No matter how difficult your circumstances may be, keep declaring to yourself, **"I WILL GET THROUGH THIS."** After making this determination, then turn towards the God given prescriptions He's given to help strengthen us and ease the pain through His word. Then finally, continue walking towards God's purpose for your life.

Yes, there will be times in life when you won't know which direction to take. Your path may become cloudy. There may be times when uncertainty concerning your future becomes overwhelming. I understand how your struggles might cause you to wonder what the future holds for you, or if God even has a purpose for your being alive.

When I was a teenager, my father taught me to sing a hymn entitled "I don't know about tomorrow." This song turned out to be my favorite hymn. The chorus to the song says, "Many things about tomorrow, I don't seem to understand, but I KNOW who holds tomorrow, and I know who holds my hand." We may not know what tomorrow holds but remember that GOD knows! You might be asking the question, "how do we know He knows?" No matter how difficult we must not allow ourselves to get stuck in the circumstances. We must understand that God's plans for us far exceed our circumstances. As you continue walking your journey, remember in the challenging times God tells us in His word, ***"For I know the plans I have for you, plans to prosper you and not to harm you, plans to give you hope and a future." Jeremiah 29:11(NIV)***

Yes, my friend, as we walk life's journey, we will all endure some pain in life just as Jesus did. But the comforting consolation is that He didn't leave us to bear it alone. No matter how much pain we endure, we are not alone, and God's plans for us remain the same. His plans for you are that you prosper spiritually, mentally, emotionally, physically, and financially! Once you arrive back to God's original plan for your life, you will rediscover all that you lost in identity, confidence, self -worth and value. My prayer for you is that after reading my story, you will find the courage, inner strength and be empowered to keep going. My prayer is that you will start seeing yourself as God sees you and begin loving yourself. If you've gotten lost on your journey in dealing with life's trials, my prayer is that God would illuminate the correct path HE wants you to take from here. My goal is to help a generation of women and perhaps men understand that you're only stuck if you choose to be stuck. You CAN make it my friend. No matter how rough your journey is, has been, or will be, always remember God STILL has awesome plans for your life! He will work out what you're going through for your good and His glory! It's never too late for a second chance. Who says you're too old? Who says it's too late? The devil is your hater and he's a liar! My friend, please don't believe the enemy's hype! Suffering, settling, and living in defeat has never been in God's plans for our lives.

Another purpose in writing is to point those of you who may be in a season of suffering to the source of strength you need. I'm aware that all who are reading may not have a relationship with God. By no means am I speaking against your beliefs, God just happens to be my higher power. He is the source of my strength. I'm simply sharing with you and acknowledging my total dependence on Him. And He's available for all who choose to trust Him. My hope is that you're encouraged to walk through your pain into a life of mental, emotional, and spiritual freedom and joy! Remember to trust the one who is the source of ALL your strength! My prayer is that you will begin taking the necessary steps to attaining the "Abundant Life" that God has already ordained for your life. My hope is that this book will remind and/or inform you that your PAIN has a purpose. It will enlighten the fact that you are not walking this journey alone. God is walking every step with you. None of what you're going through is a surprise to Him. No, my friend, God is not shocked by any hardship or pain we may endure in this life.

No matter what it looks like, feels, or seems like, remember GOD is our very present help in trouble! And as you continue reading you will be reminded of this very fact! No matter what life throws your way, be encouraged, and remember to trust God's power even when you can't trace His presence! This is the type of unshakeable faith that's described to us in Hebrews 11. This is the type of faith that God desires for His children to live by. His word tells us in (Hebrews 11:6 NIV) "And without faith it is impossible to please God, because anyone who comes to him must believe that he exists and that he rewards those that earnestly seek him."

My friend, as you journey with me into the heart of **"Purpose in the Pain,"** I'd like for you to walk in with this thought in mind; before you're able to trust in what God can do, you must FIRST believe the fact that He exists!

Chapter 2

TRUST IS A MUST

Trust in the LORD with all thine heart; And lean not unto thine own understanding. In all thy ways acknowledge him, And he shall direct thy paths. (Proverbs 3:5-6 KJV)

You've probably heard this scripture, recited it, learned it in Sunday School, Baptist Training Union, Vacation Bible School classes, and some have even learned it as a memory verse for the week. Hearing it, reciting it, and memorizing it, is one thing, but doing it, obeying, and living by it is another. Trust is a small word that carries an enormous meaning. Trust in God is different from belief. Belief means we know someone is there, but Trust implies you have no doubt that a person will help you when you need them. When a person says, "I believe you," what they're really saying is they think you are telling them the truth about a matter.

To believe is more of a temporary concept that requires one to put their faith in a person for a select period. To believe is to accept what others say about a matter as true or genuine. Trust, however, means that a person places complete confidence in another and can rely on them for anything! Trust precedes love; therefore, you can't genuinely love someone without trusting them. Trust is the foundation of love. How can you love someone and not trust them? Trust isn't something that's developed overnight. Trust is developed over time. Trust is also something that is earned through actions. Scripture tells us ***in (John 15:13 KJV), "Greater love hath no man than this, that a man lay down his life for his friends."*** Now that's love! There are people who'll quickly say, "I'll take a bullet for you." But would they really? I'm a HUGE fan of Prince and loved a song he recorded entitled "I would die 4 you". I'm not sure who the song was written for or if he really meant those words or not. But I AM sure Jesus loves me and can be trusted. I know He loves me and can be trusted not only because He's made promises to me, but most importantly because He showed me by sacrificing His LIFE for me!

When a person says they believe in God, that's different from Trusting Him. You see, we can believe God's word and yet not Trust that God will perform His word in our lives. We can believe in God, but not trust that He will answer our prayers. Trust means to have confidence in the reliability, truth, or ability of someone. If you trust someone, then they have done something which causes you to believe that they are honest and sincere and will not deliberately do anything to harm you. If you trust someone to do something, you believe that they will do it. To trust someone means that you believe they are good, honest, and effective. Trust provides intimacy and security in a relationship. It is based on integrity and honesty. Once trust is lost in a relationship it's not easy to regain. Building trust in a relationship takes commitment and hard work. I want to let you know that God CAN be trusted and when you really trust God, you have an unwavering commitment to simply lean and depend upon Him. You're not leaning on your intellect, you don't lean on your money, your education, your influence, or a connection. But instead, when you truly trust God, you're leaning and totally depending upon Him. In case you didn't know, God desires our TRUST. He wants us to trust Him for everything, and not just believe in Him for some things. Trusting God is letting go of what you think about a situation without knowing the results of what will happen. This means even when you can't see what's in front of you, trust that He is in control and will direct your path!

Another indicator that you're trusting God is when you have peace. Trust is finding peace in not knowing all the answers and surrendering all authority of a situation to Christ. No matter how things may seem, no matter how we may feel, no matter how bad it gets, and no matter how "over" it may appear to be, when you're able to have peace during chaos is when you know you're trusting God. To trust in God means to put all faith in Him to manage any situation. There's an old saying that states, "everything will work itself out." But as believers we know that things aren't simply working themselves out, but God is behind the scenes working things together for our good!

And we know that all things work together for good to them that love God, to them who are the called according to His purpose. Romans 8:28 (KJV)

My friend trusting in God means looking beyond what we see with our natural eye, and seeing by faith, what He sees. But I must be real and admit that it's not always easy to trust in the Lord. Especially when there are more bills staring you in the face than income in your bank account. When you get laid off or fired from a job, resulting in losing the little money you did have. When the doctor gives you a bad report, when you see friends and loved ones around you suffering daily from health issues, when you lose loved ones or when your marriage ends in divorce. I understand that it's not always easy to Trust God, but it's worth it to Trust Him.

Someone may be wondering, "If God is all knowing and all powerful, then why doesn't He answer all of my questions?" Someone else may be wondering, "Why is God allowing me to suffer"? Well, my friend, God isn't about quickly answering our questions for temporary relief, instead He's about taking His children through a journey to develop us. He knows if He gave us all the answers, we would have no need to strengthen our faith or trust in Him. Trusting in God is blind, however my friend, it's so necessary for us to experience true Peace and

Joy as we walk out our unknown journeys. You might also be asking the question," If I trust God does that mean I'll have no trouble? I'll have to say no, that isn't the case.

Our country has recently suffered a tremendous amount of pain and hardship. We have experienced what's called social distancing. Every church had been shut down until recently. Businesses were being ordered to close daily. State and government workers had been trained to work from home. Universities, restaurants, malls, movie theaters and gyms had all been shut down. Everyone had been ordered to stay home. Our White House leaders were at a loss. Pastors were doing their best to adjust and keep everyone encouraged, but uncertainty in their eyes had become obvious. And rightfully so, our country suffered through a pandemic with no cure. Hundreds of thousands of people have been both negatively affected by the pandemic, and so many have died due to hardships from the pandemic. Life had become extremely different and so uncertain. The unemployment rate across the country had peaked to an all-time high of 14.7 percent and I also fell into that statistic. Without having employment I've had many days of waking up with a huge question mark hanging over my head. Things had been rough and uncertain for so many in one way or another during the pandemic. And there are those like me who even dealt with struggles before the pandemic. This had only escalated hardships for some. Although we thought things had gotten a little better, we as a country and some individually are still dealing with some negative effects from the pandemic. Although things have gotten a little better over time, we have all been forced to adjust our lives to a "new normal". You see, this was a situation that no one had the answers to in the beginning and two years later there are still no concrete answers or solutions.

We are all doing the best we can do with the knowledge that we do have. And yet those of us who believe in God must continue to trust Him. That's really all we can do. I'm grateful to God for keeping me and my loved ones safe thus far during the crisis. All my needs have been met. Sadly, there are those who are not able to say the same. So many lives have been negatively touched and lost as a direct result of the 2020 pandemic. These situations can cause so many questions to arise in your mind. But we must continue to trust that God is working to accomplish HIS purpose even when we don't understand. As bad and frightening as this situation has been, God even has a purpose in allowing this crisis. No, I'm not saying He caused it, but I do believe He allowed it.

He's sovereign, and it couldn't have happened without HIS permission. Because He's God He may choose to never reveal His purpose for allowing so much pain. There were plenty of negative events that transpired in our country during 2020 and 2021. It was enough to get everyone's attention whether they took heed or not. From the oldest to the youngest, from the richest to the poorest, every denomination, color, and gender. We were all affected. Our lives were interrupted in a major way. I don't profess to have the answers, but it is my belief that God wanted our attention. It's my belief that He wanted us to recognize our need for Him. Not because He's an arrogant God or needs His ego stroked, but because He's a loving God who knows we need Him. Without forcing himself on us, He gives us choices to make. This crisis that we've endured and come through has certainly drawn me closer to God. Therefore, if all I've done is gotten closer to God during this pandemic that's MORE than enough. Since I'm still alive I'll continue to encourage myself by affirming as I've learned to do through all negative circumstances that, "I'm coming out of this BETTER than I was before!" Sometimes we may have to cry and may not understand why things happen the way they do, but even behind the questions and tears continue reminding yourself that, "God has allowed this for a GOOD purpose!" The only way this can be done is by trusting God.

As I stated before, trusting in God means more than merely believing who He is. Trusting in the Lord means to have confidence in Him. When we choose to trust God, it doesn't mean life no longer has difficulties, but instead that we can face those difficulties without fear and that we can remain confident in His power to carry us through them all! You see it's easy to say that we trust God when everything is good, and all is going according to plan. But will you trust God when things aren't good and going according to plan? To trust God means we must allow Him to do what He wants to do without any help from us. To trust God is to be able to say," Lord I'm going to let you do what you think is best, and I won't fear the outcome." My friend, trust and belief in God go hand in hand. To trust in God is to first believe that He is real and then be willing to surrender everything to Him. We must get to the place in our relationship with God where we can and say, "not my will but your will be done." If things don't happen as quickly as we think they ought, we must trust that His timing is perfect, and that He has a purpose for the delay. I came to the realization that the only way I would make it through my painful situations in life was to trust in the only one who could help me. Even when it felt like God wasn't there, I trusted that He was. I'm a living witness of the fact that He won't ever leave you alone in your circumstance. I encourage you to keep on trusting Him no matter what! You might be asking the question, why should I trust God?

Here are some reasons why we SHOULD and CAN trust God just to name a few:

We can trust God because He's sovereign meaning He has supreme power. We can trust God because He's a good father. We can trust Him because He's a faithful God. We can trust God because He loves us unconditionally. We should trust Him because He knew us BEFORE He formed us in our mothers' wombs. We can trust Him because He's all-knowing. God is not surprised by what we're going through. We can trust Him because He's always with us. God cares about what we're going through! God has the power to change what we're going through!!

He has the power to strengthen us in our struggles. God uses our struggles to change us for the better. God's love for us never changes. God's grace to us is sufficient!

God's mercies to us are new every morning! Now who wouldn't Trust a God like that?

Chapter 3

REJOICE IN THE PAIN

(James 1:2-4 NIV) reads Consider it pure joy, my brothers, and sisters, whenever you face trials of many kinds, 3. Because you know that the testing of your faith produces perseverance. 4. Let perseverance finish its work so that you may be mature and complete not lacking anything.

In this passage of scripture James encourages us to consider it pure joy when faced with trials of many kinds. If you'll notice, he said "When" and not "If." Why? Because he knew that trials are inevitable. From James' point of view, we are to expect trials understanding that we will all suffer in this life. There's an old saying written by the poet Henry Wadsworth Longfellow in 1841 which states, "Into each life some rain must fall." Jesus said to His disciples in ***(John 16:33 NIV), "In this world you WILL have trouble."*** According to this promise, I think we can all agree that none of us will or can escape troubles in this life. This is a promise that's clear and sometimes overlooked. But it doesn't end there, it's followed by another promise which says, ***"But take heart! I have overcome the world."*** This promise is filled with hope!

Suffering is not something we should be surprised about or even resent as believers. We must understand that we are not exempt from having difficult moments in life. Knowing this helps us face suffering without any false hopes. Pain will come, but remember pain has a purpose in our lives. The bible doesn't give us one specific reason we suffer.

The truth is we may never know the full reason. But James encourages us to rejoice when facing trials of many kinds. Therefore, even when we have those, "When it rains, it pours" moments in life, James encourages us that, even then, we ought to rejoice. Why should we rejoice? How can we rejoice? We're able to rejoice because we know there's something else! We can rejoice because we know there's potential in our pain! Even though your situation may be uncomfortable, something about it could produce something great! Responding in Joy doesn't mean we enjoy suffering. We respond in Joy for what suffering can produce, which is perseverance, maturity, and wisdom. We must believe that something deeper than we can see with our natural eye is going on. James knows that trials test our faith. Suffering reveals what we genuinely believe in for our hope and strength. As we continue trusting Him through our trials, our faith grows! Suffering results in spiritual maturity. It helps us grow stronger and mature in our faith. Suffering makes us humbler, empathetic, compassionate, and sensitive to the needs of others who may suffer.

Therefore, from God's perspective, our growing stronger in Him and maturing in our faith is far more important than our not experiencing pain and hardship.

PAIN STRENGTHENS YOUR FAITH

When you're going through a season of suffering, I understand how it may be difficult to see how any good can come from it. But it does. Remember, your trials are only tests. God allows us to endure suffering and then uses that suffering to strengthen our faith. You may be asking, "Why can't He just give us stronger faith?" My friend, stronger faith must be earned. And the only way that lasting unshakable faith can be earned is through tests and trials. My father used to sing a beautiful song entitled "Through it all", written by the late Andre Crouch. There is a verse in the song which says:

"I thank God for the mountains, and I thank Him for the valleys, I thank Him for the storms He brought me through, for if I'd never had a problem, I wouldn't know that God could solve them, I'd never know what **FAITH** in God could do."

Experiencing times of pain and struggle is the perfect time to turn towards God. It will push you to talk with Him like never before. As we confide in Him and begin spending more intimate time with Him, He begins to reveal His power in our lives. As we continue trusting Him through the trials, our faith in Him grows. As a runner gains endurance through running another mile, we as believers also gain the ability to trust God through every trial.

The chorus to the song 'Through it all' says, "Through it all, through it all, I've learned to trust in Jesus, I've learned to trust in God, through it all, through it all, I've learned to depend upon His word." As God helps you through every trial it will cause your trust and faith in Him to grow.

Experiencing trials is how something beneficial happens in the life of a believer. We don't have to fret because the testing of our faith is NOT meant to harm us, it's meant to benefit us! The benefit is that we develop something while in the trial that we would not have developed without trials!

We are encouraged to consider going through hardships in life as "Joyful", because trials and pain help us develop a deeper trust in God. In all areas of life, growth only comes through overcoming difficulty. James points out that we shouldn't try to avoid trials, but instead make the most of them because by faith you know that the testing of our faith produces perseverance. Therefore, my friend, as we continue to trust God through our trials, we are letting perseverance finish its work. The more our faith is tested, the more perseverance is produced. I wonder how many are reaching for perfection and complete maturity? Perfection-Complete maturity is only found in perfect faith in

God. To receive the benefits of maturing through our trials, we must first acknowledge that God has allowed the trials for our benefit. If we don't acknowledge that, we will miss an opportunity to grow. Satan wants to use trials to weaken and discourage us, but God wants to use them to strengthen and complete us. Don't be deceived by the enemy. Don't get lost in the circumstances of what you're going through. As I stated before, there may be times when we won't understand what God is doing. There will be times He may not give us all the details, but remember when He doesn't is an opportunity for us to place our complete trust in Him. When we do this our faith is being strengthened!

PAIN STRENGTHENS YOUR ENDURANCE and PERSEVERANCE

When storms of adversity and doubt come, we must hold on tight to God's promises and trust that He's still with us. Isn't it encouraging to find throughout His word that we serve a God who keeps His promises! Holding on to His word will help us persevere with hope as we wait for God to carry out His promises in our lives. The same way we work on our muscles in a gym, this type of waiting is an opportunity to develop our spiritual muscles. We do so by making a deliberate decision to incorporate God's Word in our daily lives and to have faith that God is working on our behalf! As we make the choice to Trust His promises, our hope grows, and we learn to face times of difficulty with expectant endurance!

God doesn't need to see how strong we are. He's already aware of our strength level.

Experiencing pain is an opportunity for us to see how strong we are. Sometimes we are so quick to put a limit on ourselves and say what we can or can't do, not realizing the strength we really have. Although we don't like pain, pain is the only way to truly discover just how strong you really are in Christ. In fact, I think I'd be safe in saying, people don't hate pain, what they hate is pain without a purpose. I'm sure you've heard the phrase, "Perspective is everything." Well, if we would just stand back and take a different perspective on our pain, it won't take the pain away, but it will give purpose to our pain.

Think about people getting tattoos. This process is an example of experiencing pain with purpose. I know that the process of getting a tattoo is painful. Although painful, it's not the pain that you're focused on when getting a tattoo, but instead it's the outcome. No matter how extremely painful and uncomfortable the process is the excitement over the process keeps you in the chair or on the table. I can remember several years ago working out with my personal trainer. During my workout routine he would sometimes stack weight on the machines that I was sure I couldn't manage. Before he even asked me to lift the weight, I had begun rolling my eyes and shaking my head saying NO. I even got angry with him for expecting me to be able to lift the weight with my arms and legs. But my apprehension and frustration didn't cause him to let up. He continued instructing me to lift the designated weight. As I attempted to lift, although difficult and painful with his push and my perseverance I did it. The next time I lifted the weight I noticed it was a bit easier and even easier the next time! I noticed that the easier it got the more weight he added.

Why? Because through lifting the weight I was building up my endurance and strengthening my perseverance. Lifting heavy weight causes your muscles to grow so that you're able to lift heavier weight. In the same way, when you're tested through the fires of pain in life your endurance is expanded. As your endurance expands, so does your perseverance. You'll find yourself able to take more and go further. To persevere simply means to hang in there.

My friend, pain serves an awesome purpose in our lives. Experiencing pain stretches our ability to persevere through the most difficult circumstances. You see, as much as we'd rather skip pain in our lives, there is no way to grow or become stronger without it. I can recall after working out consistently, I noticed progress in my target areas. When I first started my workout journey, it wasn't easy. There were days I fought getting out of bed, but I pressed through it. Then I began seeing progress. The more progress I noticed, the more pain I was willing to endure. Seeing the progress from those rough days of working out caused me to continue to persevere! Why?

Because I knew something good was coming from it. We ought not look at life from a perspective of pain, but instead see our pain through a perspective of PURPOSE! Pain will come, but pain has a purpose in our lives! We can fight the pain or allow that pain to promote us to purpose. **Pain has a purpose to help us fulfill a GREATER purpose!** In your suffering try to see that God may be doing something in you before He does something through you. The difficulty you're going through right now is not without purpose. The purpose for your struggles may not always be physically visible, but there is a purpose. My friend, remember, pain strengthens our faith muscles. Pain and struggle both give us strength to soar! But you'll never get there if you avoid the pain in your life. Numbing the pain with drugs, alcohol, sex etc., will get you nowhere. You must PUSH through your pain.

Everyone wants to be Joseph in the palace with everything going well, but no one wants to be Joseph in the pit. But, Joseph's pain from the pit served a purpose. You see, Joseph was betrayed by his family. He was thrown into a pit by his brothers. He was made a slave and falsely accused by his boss's wife. Joseph was treated unfairly. But after experiencing a tremendous amount of pain, Joseph was later promoted to the palace! However, he had to go through some *painful* things in order to get there. It was through the pain he suffered where he developed the strength enough to end up declaring in Genesis 50, "What Satan meant for evil, God turned to GOOD!"

Just as God caused something good to come from Joseph's pain, He will do the same for us if we would respond the correct way. This is the mindset James had when he said to count it all Joy when going through trials of many kinds. Our response as believers should be different from the world. You see, the world hates suffering and will do their best to run from suffering or prevent it. But James is instructing Christians to respond in a different way. Sometimes God just needs to toughen us up. Sometimes we can be too stubborn, too hardheaded, too spoiled, too fearful, or timid. Some can be too puffed up and full of themselves. Or sometimes God may just simply want more of us. I don't have the answers as to why we go through our individual sufferings, but one thing for sure is that He knows what we need. What's happening in our lives might be a mystery to us, but nothing is a mystery to God. He's aware of our past, present, and future. Sometimes, we might ask God why? And although He understands why, He may not always give us the answers. And we must trust His judgment on that decision. We should also remember in times of suffering that it's not God's responsibility to tell us why these things are happening. God knows that there are some things in life that are way beyond our comprehension. He knows what we are capable of handling.

Therefore, getting angry with God is not the answer. We must trust His word written in (Isaiah 55:8 NIV) which states, ***"For my thoughts are not your thoughts, and neither are your ways my ways," declares the Lord.*** It's important to remember that God is a good and loving Father. Please also remember that having trouble, pain, hardship, and suffering does not mean that your life doesn't matter to God. Whatever He allows in our lives, it is our job to trust Him and learn to respond the correct way. No matter what we face in life, our Heavenly Father loves us, cares for us and His promises to us are still intact. Another crucial point to remember is that God doesn't allow us to go through suffering without a purpose in mind.

James encourages us to have joy in the face of trials, why? Because trials lead to perseverance and perseverance leads to *maturity*! James is encouraging us to embrace trials because they lead us into maturing into the type of Christians that God created us to be. James says to let perseverance finish. Let it be completed. Don't interrupt what God is doing through your trials. It's not that we should enjoy trials, but we can be joyful over the outcome of them in our lives. We can be joyful knowing that God does not waste our pain. It's through the times that test us where we're able to draw closer to God and experience more of Him. Therefore, it's not about the struggle itself, but instead the result of the hardship. It's our duty as believers not to complain through our tests and trials, but consider what God is doing through the trials. My friend, don't back down, don't run, or try to avoid trials, but instead stand strong and persevere!

To persevere means to bear up through extremely difficult circumstances. **Perseverance is being able to see things through to the end. Perseverance is the ability to keep moving towards a goal and overcoming pain, setbacks, and disappointments that could not have been seen at the outset.** We can stand strong during tests and trials knowing that all things are working for our good. Your suffering is not in vain my friend. God has a purpose!

Remember, we find out what we're really made of during times of tests and trials. No matter how rough your times of hardship may be, keep this thought in mind, "Trials produce perseverance and perseverance produces character"! Are you getting the picture? It's all working for your good!

Chapter 4

THE PAIN OF DIVORCE

My friend, as we continue our journey, take a peek with me if you will into my former life as a Pastor's wife aka "First lady." 2007 was a very trying year for me. It was the year of my divorce from a man I had spent almost 20 years of my life with. In 2004, life as I had known it began taking a drastic turn for the worse. The turn came slowly and out of nowhere it seemed, but once it began it snowballed quickly. As with all marriages, some days were good, and others were bad. It's been said that "If you can get through the first five years of your marriage, then you can make it. Well, we had done that, so according to that statement we were good. We had moved to a different state, expanded our family, and had gotten to a beautiful place it seemed. Then there came a major shift. It had gotten to the point where things were very strange in my marriage to say the least. Over the years some have asked, "You were with him so long, why not just stay?" There have been times when I've asked myself the same question. Things had seemed to work for so long. We were both Christians. We were both Pastors children aka PK's. We had produced three beautiful children together.

For a period, things looked and felt perfect for us, however, things are not always as they appear. It is my belief that being unequally yoked is a sure way for a marriage to suffer. Over the years I learned that being equally yoked involves more than simply two people being Christians. It means two sharing the same values and beliefs. It means two people walking together. Simply put, being equally yoked means being compatible. How can you be yoked to someone who's not going in the same direction? How can you be equally yoked to someone who sees things different than you? It was during our last rough patch together when it became noticeably clear to me that we were unequally yoked. I had seen things over the years but chose to brush them under a rug and persevere as though they would disappear over time. Although with God's grace my marriage worked for many years even with being on different pages, when it was time for us to really be connected, walk, and fight together as one, we couldn't do it and as a result my marriage didn't stand. I've often asked myself, "Why didn't my marriage work?" Some may be asking, "But aren't you a Christian?" Others may be asking, "Weren't you married to a pastor?" The answer is yes, I am a Christian and he is a pastor. But what some don't seem to realize is that being a Christian does NOT make you exempt from experiencing trouble, adversity, pain or even divorce as some may think. We will all suffer in this life. I'd be lying if I said my marriage was all bad because it wasn't. I was blessed to be able to experience some good times, but the bad times had begun to overshadow the good times. Early in my marriage we had some major struggles, but pressed through those struggles. However, this time was different. Being public figures in a small city also made the details of our marital struggles and divorce very public and even more painful. This was very painful not only for me to endure but also for my children who were young at the time. I prayed many days that our situation would not turn my children away from God, but instead draw them to God. My marriage ending was a rough period in my life to say the least. It was a very crushing and humiliating experience. Divorce is an extremely complicated process within itself, but imagine if you will, having the private details of your marital struggles and divorce become public. This is how it was for me, and this added even more pain to my situation. The painful situation my family lived through had become the latest soap opera in our city during that time. There were those who I believe prayed sincerely for us, but many people laughed, gossiped, pointed fingers, and took sides instead of praying for us. During that time, I watched good people with good hearts walk away from the ministry.

Over the years I've noticed how so many women are attracted to the "glory" that comes with being a pastor's wife aka "First Lady". The special public attention a Pastor's wife receives in the African American church can be very appealing. All eyes are on her and her family because she's attached to the Pastor. The role of a Pastor's wife can give you feelings of being "the Queen of the house." It can come with many perks such as security, special parking, special seating, an entourage of those appointed to serve, gifts, and many acts of kindness from the church membership etc. But what so many don't seem to take into consideration is the "story behind the glory." While the role comes with special benefits and feelings of prestige, the role can also cause you to become isolated and live your life in a bubble. Pastors are many times gazed upon and treated as rock stars. It takes an extraordinarily strong woman to walk in the shoes as "First Lady". The role is not always what it's cracked up to be. Not all situations of a Pastor's wife are the same, but in many instances as mine, being a Pastor's wife places her on a pedestal that may or may not be her desire, but comes with the territory. For some, this life can be attractive and a major desire. So much so, that many have gone after the role at all costs. Some women have even sat back and set their sights on the role of being a Pastor's wife even while that Pastor is already married. It's the position and attention that some may be attracted to, but sis, be mindful and prayerful that your choices and desires line up with God's will. Don't get me wrong, being a Pastor's wife can be a beautiful experience, but like everything it does come with its challenges. Because what many don't seem to realize is that no matter how perfect someone's life appears to be, NO ONE has a perfect problem free life. Not even the "First Lady". When two imperfect people unite, how can they have a perfect marriage? It's not possible my friend. But what is possible is for two imperfect people to honor God in their union by inviting His presence from the very beginning and choosing to work together as one. In looking back, I realized this was something that didn't happen in the beginning for me. No this isn't something I'm proud of, but it's something I'm choosing to share to prayerfully help someone else.

Taking on this perspective has helped me tremendously in understanding how something that was once beautiful can take such an enormous turn.

My friend, no matter what age or gender you are, whether you desire to be wife of a Pastor, wife of a construction worker, or even if you're a man desiring to be a husband, I urge you NOT to enter marriage without thinking clearly and involving God in your decision from the very beginning. In looking back, I realize that getting married at 19 was too young to make such a major decision. At 19 you're not even sure who YOU are, and it's important to know you before giving yourself to someone else who's also trying to find themselves. Without thinking clearly, while trying to find myself and discover my dreams, I took on an enormous role of helping someone else fulfill their dreams. That was not the best decision, but God's grace was sufficient during that time.

Marriage is a lifelong commitment. And if entered haphazardly you'll find yourself using your entire marriage trying to fix what was broken from the very start. ALL things should be considered when making such a huge decision. I can recall my father who was also my Pastor, asking me a question during his counseling me before I got married. He asked me, "Have you seen him angry?" At the time I felt that was the silliest thing. I thought, "Why do I need to see him angry before marrying him?" That was the thinking process of a 19-year-old girl. I'm sure my father asked that question because he knew how important it was to know ALL sides of a person BEFORE marriage when making such a serious commitment. But just like our Heavenly Father, he didn't force his decision on me, but allowed me the freedom to make my own decision. But he certainly didn't allow it without ALL knowing how he felt. During the ceremony when asked "Who giveth this woman to be married to this man," my father answered, "I Rev. Fredrick E. Wilson

Sr., with mixed emotions, give my daughter to be married to this man." We laughed for many years about how audacious his response was, but he would always say with sincerity, "I meant every word." It was after getting married when I did begin to see some things that had I seen before I'm sure I would have made a different decision. But honestly there were things I did see, but because of pride and shame of moving too fast chose to ignore them as though they would go away. Although I was aware of some things that didn't gel with me, I stayed. I stayed because I felt that staying in the situation was my consequence for moving too fast. I was young and didn't personally know much about God's amazing grace and mercy at that time. Therefore, I'd made up my mind that I would stay and do my best to" make it work", as so many others have attempted to do.

I went into the marriage with one understanding of my role as wife and that was to be a "helpmate." Although young and immature, even then I was aware of my worth. Not knocking anyone,

but I always knew that God had placed more inside of me than to only be a hat/lap cloth wearing, second row/pulpit sitting, artificial smiling "First Lady". He'd gifted me with talents that heavily enhanced his assignment as Pastor. Before we had gotten married, the church he pastored lacked a thriving music ministry. A thriving music ministry plays a huge role in the growth of a church. Therefore, he asked me to help him in this area and I gladly accepted because it's something I loved to do. On the surface it appeared to be a match made in heaven. I'd used those gifts to help my father who was also a pastor, so surely this would be an impressive duo in marriage and ministry I thought. This just reiterates my point about the age19 being a bit too young to make such important decisions. I went on to perform my duties in ministry along with being a wife and mother.

> From the very start, ministry together was a part of my marriage. Not to toot my own horn, but the fact is as time went on, both music ministries of the church's my former husband

pastored began to thrive under my tutelage as music director. The music ministries grew from just a few members to choir stands overflowing with members to the point where he'd begun exploring ideas of expanding to accommodate the major growth within the music ministry and church. God had begun opening so many opportunities for the music ministry at that time including singing for the governor's inaugural ceremony. Many people who had joined the church were drawn there by hearing the music ministry. Many musicians would sit in our rehearsals just to listen because the music ministry had become the best in the city. We'd began preparation for recording, but as time went on it never happened.

BUMPS IN THE ROAD

Later in my marriage, I noticed how different our mindsets were. Things I'd noticed in the beginning had become more prevalent. There seemed to always be a struggle when preparing music for worship. During that time, I began noticing episodes of arguments at home about song choices, open arguments in band rehearsals about what I'd taught the musician, along with public gestures of his disapproval during worship services, etc. Some of the instances would bring me to silent and sometimes open tears. The gestures weren't only noticed by me but had become something noticeable to everyone. These situations had become very humiliating and embarrassing to endure. One of the very things about me that I loved to do and considered to be a major help and asset to him he came to resent. There were times when directing the choir, he would suddenly stop us as though it was a move of the Holy spirit. Of course, you can never argue with authority, however I've always suspected that those times were malicious moves towards me. I can also recall leading our first women's ministry meeting. I had been extremely nervous about conducting the meeting because it was my first time leading a ministry other than the music ministry.

Excited about how well things had gone, I couldn't wait to get home and share the news with him. When I told him how well things had gone, to my surprise, his response was, "It couldn't have been that good, I wasn't there." Although by that time I was well aware of the inflated ego, that response still left me in total shock. Looking for his approval and encouragement as my pastor and husband at that time, my spirit was crushed, and my confidence was shaken by the response.

His approval was very important to me; however, his approval had become something that was nonexistent during that time. I noticed even more strange incidents. One Sunday after worship I remember asking his opinion about how he felt music had gone that day. It was the beginning of a new year, and we were implementing some new structure in worship. As music director it was my responsibility to lead worship alone on this Sunday while developing the new structure. I was a bit nervous because I'd never led the praise and worship period alone, but God was there in the midst of the service. In my opinion, the hearts of the people had been adequately prepared for receiving the word of God. But when asking his opinion of how things went, the shocking response was, "It was alright, but they don't come to hear you sing, they come to hear me preach". Once again, my spirit was broken. Those responses revealed some things that over the years I never wanted to admit were there. There appeared to have been some intimidation present in these responses. What had definitely become apparent was that there were some inward insecurities there. These types of responses caused me to walk on pins and needles being careful to never overstep his authority. Not fully understanding the cause of the insecurities and triggers, I was hindered most times from fully operating in the gifts God had placed upon my life. Of course the insecurities and intimidation were never verbally expressed to me, but his actions had become much louder than his words.

I've learned that many times insecurity can be masked with ego and pride, which is what I endured on many occasions. And with each incident, my confidence as his wife and partner in ministry was stripped more. I went from being a strong confident young woman to a broken, insecure and unsure "first lady" second guessing my every move.

You see my friend; it was never a competition for me. It brought me joy to prepare the music ministry to soften the ground for receiving the word of God. I considered what we did together as teamwork making the dream-work. However, those responses sounded very egotistical, and I didn't quite know how to deal with it. Once while visiting another ministry, after observing us work together with my leading music to prepare for his preaching, the pastor described our marriage and ministry together as the head and neck working together. I recall a time when he agreed with that seasoned pastor's description of us working as a team, but with every negative act and comment it was clear that he had a different viewpoint. Everything I had ever done musically while married was always with him in mind. My job in worship entailed preparing the congregation to receive the word of God from him. It was never about me, myself and I.

As time went on, I was removed from all duties as Music director. There were changes being made and he'd expressed his desire for me to sit next to him. He then began expressing his desire for me to no longer sing in "his church". My life has been music from my birth. Whether singing, teaching, directing or listening, music brings me Joy. My comfort zone is in music, but it appeared that I was being stripped of doing what I loved. I couldn't understand all that was happening. It was a crazy time, and what I did know is that my marriage was suffering. I had also noticed that these extreme changes occurred during the time some truth regarding his inappropriate behavior within the church had been revealed. Some of that inappropriate behavior had occurred with my assistant to be exact. I couldn't understand why I then had become his enemy in his mind. I really can't make sense of it, but it was clear that we were no longer on one accord. This was so strange and mind boggling to me. This was also a very heartbreaking, confusing, and horrific time in my life.

There was another strange incident that occurred during a church service after I had been instructed to, "not to sing again in his church". Things weren't well at home, but I'd mustered up enough energy to attend church. This time there happened to be a visiting minister there. As I sat listening to the Caucasian gentleman known as "The Prophet," he began walking towards me as he spoke. He weirdly addressed me asking if I would sing a song. I had never met him and was a bit shaken by his request. I looked at him, smiled and held my head down with no response. He then asked me again, but only this time after asking me, he then pointed the microphone towards my mouth attempting to force an answer. Keeping in mind what I had been told at home, I didn't quite know how to respond. After a few seconds I smiled and answered, "no, I'm sorry I can't." This was the most uncomfortable, embarrassing, mortifying shameful, demeaning, cringe worthy, degrading, and crushing position I'd ever endured. And it didn't stop there. The guest minister then asked me why I couldn't sing. I remember my heart beating so fast that I began to perspire. You see, I didn't want to appear that I was being disobedient to the "man of God." And neither did I want to later deal with friction at home from my disobeying his wishes as "Pastor" which was something at home he often reminded me he was. We were both on display at that time, and what was I to do? With everyone staring at me quietly as they listened, and the microphone still in my mouth, before I knew it, I responded, "Because he doesn't want me to." He had expressed his desire for me to no longer sing in "his church". I've often thought if there was something different I could have done during that moment. I guess I could have covered the weird scene by smiling and agreeing to sing for the guest minister, but again I would have also risked being accused of disobeying his rules as pastor. Therefore, I chose to be honest and let the chips fall where they may. My friend, are you feeling the struggle here? Still, the visiting minister didn't stop. He then addressed him by asking if what I was saying was true, and of course at that moment his answer was no.

After the minister received his permission, I did walk up to sing, however, never did due to a prolonged altar call which was led by my former husband. I'm sure this all sounds like a crazy movie to you, but trust me, experiencing it was more like a nightmare. By this time, we had become a laughingstock in our city and this incident added even more pain, and gossip to our situation. Thus, causing the atmosphere in our home to become even more dismal, confusing, and toxic. Considering all that had transpired, I couldn't for the life of me understand why or how the stance of "silencing me" came into play. My guess is that he thought I would perhaps hurt him in public out of my pain, which is something I would have never done. My friend, there were so many bizarre things happening at that time, I just couldn't make sense of them all. But one thing I know for certain is that it was a very painful time in my life.

Towards the end of my marriage many things happened that caused my mind to spin. Things occurred that pierced my heart and caused me to question myself. I began to question everyone around me. There were things that transpired during that time that made me feel I was crazy, but deep down inside I knew I wasn't. Things such as finding out rumors that had been spread were not only rumors, but were in fact true, almost sent me over the edge. You see, prior to these events, details of his inappropriate behavior could be found in letters that were placed on windshields of every car after leaving worship services. Each letter distributed contained names of different women he had allegedly been inappropriate with. While all of the rumors may not have been true, because some of them were, I questioned them all. The letters began surfacing so much, there were jokes being made from some of his staff about the letters referring to them as "volume three or four" being available to read that day. While others joked, my heart was being torn apart with each "volume" (letter). During this time, my private financial information also began to surface in letters for everyone to see. Can you imagine copies of all of your private bank statements circulating for all to see? I'd begun to feel so unprotected and violated. Small things such as making a trip to the grocery store had become a major chore. I didn't want to speak to anyone. I no longer felt up to faking a smile. I no longer knew what was true and what was false in my marriage or in the church. When asking him what was going on and if anything spoken in the letters were true, it was all denied. He claimed to have no knowledge about what was happening, or what had been written. His answer was always, "The devil is just attacking". But something just didn't feel right. The more I asked questions, the more hostile he became and the more I was being made to feel as though I was delusional. I was constantly told I was listening to the wrong people, and that my relationship with God was off. I purchased many books at that time to help keep my sanity and to make sure my relationship with God stayed intact. All of this began cutting away at my confidence. I wanted so desperately to believe him, but with every denial I'd begun feeling more disturbed. It is a very lonely place to live your life in a fishbowl with everyone watching your every move. That is the life of a Pastor, his wife and family. When you live this type of life your circle of true friends are very small. And as rumors and drama grew my small circle of friends began to shrink even more. People don't seem to realize the Pastors, wives and their families are human, and they hurt and bleed like everyone else. With everything that was happening I didn't know what or how to feel. He had somehow convinced himself that everyone was against him. At that time, the phrase "The devil is attacking" was used so much that it sickens me even today to hear the phrase. This was his answer whenever more rumors or trouble surfaced during that time.

I've found that many times, it's not the enemy causing havoc in our lives, but instead our own poor choices that we must own up to.

One afternoon while home trying to grasp it all mentally and emotionally, my doorbell rang. It was an older member of the church who had come by for the purpose of convincing me to stay and not walk away. She had been a very influential member for many years. She was the member who was known by everyone for her skill in raising substantial amounts of money for special days, particularly Pastors anniversaries. This woman had also been known as the alleged "mistress" of the former pastor. As I listened and realized where her conversation was going, I, not politely, but immediately showed her my front door. I then proceeded to close the door firmly behind her. I thought, "the nerve of her"! I kept thinking "Why in the world would she think I'd take counsel from her of all people?" There were so many things that transpired, things that just didn't make a lot of sense so much so, I began questioning everything and everybody. I even began questioning myself. I was certain he had given her permission to come to my home in hopes that she could influence my decision of staying instead of walking away. By this time, my trust had been shattered. I'm sure my distaste for all that was transpiring was felt by both he and the church. My presence at the church had become slim to none. It seemed the more we tried to work things out, the worse things got. It was a very difficult time not only for my family, but also for the church family. During this time, many key members of the church began walking away which caused me to become even more skeptical. Due to the stress of the situation, I'd lost a tremendous amount of weight to the point of not recognizing myself in the mirror.

Then to make matters worse, during our family trauma, the church's building project was also in motion. The major growth of the church had caused them to begin having three services per Sunday and this matter consumed his mind 24/7. But as important as I knew this matter was, our marriage was simultaneously falling apart, and to me, our marriage and family were more important and worth saving. Therefore, following many months of struggle, I asked him if he would be willing to take some time off to focus on our marriage and family. I wanted this because I felt the marriage and family unit slipping away. The home was becoming colder and nothing other than the building was being addressed. After pleading with him to take a much needed sabbatical for our family, his response was, **"No I can't! God told me to build this building in SPITE of my wife and family!"** That response was shocking and heartbreaking for me to say the least. When reflecting, I can still hear those words ring in my ear today. He had chosen his job over our marriage and family. There is one thing I'll never do and that is to argue with anyone about their God and their beliefs. But I will defend the God I believe in. And my belief is that the God I serve would never make giving attention to a "building project" or brick and mortar more important than giving MUCH needed attention to your hurting marriage and family. The response to me meant that the church had taken priority over the state of our marriage and family. My response to his crushing statement was, "You can have your new church, but one day you'll have the church and no family". I was hurt, crushed, angry, devastated, and disappointed by the response. At that point I no longer wanted to be attached to or hurt by the narcissistic superior behavior. I proceeded to ask myself,

"what's left?" And then I thought, "Why stay?" You see, by the time the church was built, the membership had dwindled tremendously. The need for a 100-seat choir stand was no longer necessary because the membership had fallen. But even so, his decision was to remain focused on a "building project" instead of his hurting marriage and family.

In trying to work through my marriage, there was a time when a "seasoned" First Lady counseled me. Her advice to me was to "Just stay, take your corner and let him have his." These were her exact words. I thought," who wants to live in a corner"? She also advised me with pride I might add, by saying "No matter who might be with him behind closed doors, you will be the only one who's able to stand when they call for his wife". The sad thing about this to me is that she said this as though it was something for me to take pride in. This is how so many have chosen to handle their situations. However, living in a corner to have peace and joy and settling for my name (as the Mrs.) to be called in public was not exciting to me. Then another seasoned "first lady" advised me to "stay for the stuff." She shared her pain of being a victim of ongoing infidelity with me and advised me to make him pay by accepting and demanding his material gifts. Her exact words were, "make him pay." When I asked her how she dealt with her husband mistakes with membership, she shared how she used her husband's mistress to get what she wanted. That pastor's wife used her husband's mistakes and his mistress to her advantage. That was her way of coping and easing her pain.

Although I had many thoughts of ways to get revenge, doing so would not have brought me any true peace of mind. Manipulating the situation by making him pay for his actions through showers of gifts was not enough for me. I was looking for true remorse. Remorse is more than simply saying "I'm sorry" for the moment. True remorse is demonstrated. True remorse is acknowledging you've hurt someone and are willing to give them the adequate time for healing no matter how long it takes. True remorse shows you're sorry for your actions and true remorse is something I never saw. I needed someone who loved me enough to allow me the time needed to heal. What I wanted was unity in our marriage. But instead, my marriage had gotten very toxic. It had become apparent that the only way my marriage would work is if I continued dimming my light to make him feel secure. You see my friend, it was not the inappropriate behavior only that hurt, it was feeling as though I and my children were not important enough to give the necessary attention for healing. I realized that the only way to live in harmony was to do it his way or no way. I knew this was not how I wanted to live the rest of my life. Therefore, after much prayer and realizing we were not on the same page in many ways, it was clear that staying in the marriage was not the answer for me. When your marriage becomes a constant source of pain, that's a major problem that can't be ignored. When the respect in your marriage is lost, that's also a problem that can't be ignored and MUST be addressed. Ultimately, when your marriage is no longer glorifying God or bringing you joy, what's left? My marriage was no longer doing either. And after many attempts of trying to save the marriage, the marriage died.

In criticism of my decision to walk away and divorce, some have said, "You know God doesn't condone divorce." My response to that criticism was, "And neither does He condone a lie, but His grace is sufficient." I made the decision that was best for me, and trusted God with all of the details.

In my reflection over the years and adjusting to the death of my marriage, I've experienced many mental and emotional roller coasters. Those mental and emotional roller coasters led to physical roller coasters as well. I've made several moves in trying to adjust and cope with starting life all over again. I've experienced times of looking at my children's sad faces and wondering if I had done the right thing by walking away. Sometimes the enemy will cause you to question your own decision, especially during times of struggle. Believe me, during those times he took every opportunity he could to remind me of what I had materialistically before walking away. You see, I had lived in a 7500 sq. ft. home with five bedrooms, seven bathrooms and three car garage that sat on a private lake. We owned a Mercedes, Navigator, Lexus, and Ford explorer. We had been blessed to the point of giving away my Lexus to one of the church members. Our home was the most beautiful on the block. My children and I wore the best clothing, and I was a stay-at-home mom/wife. I had traveled the world inclusive of Aruba, Hawaii, The Holy Land, Egypt, Jamaica, and the Bahamas just to name a few. Our church had become one of if not the largest African American church in the city. I was living the perfect life, right? It may have appeared that way from the surface, but it turned out to be far from the truth. While I loved my former husband, our beautiful family, our home, the church, and was very appreciative of the things we had acquired together in marriage, living a lavish lifestyle with no peace in my home was not how I wanted to live the rest of my life. I know many women who would give anything to live that type of lavish lifestyle, not realizing that many times there is a price to pay in living that lifestyle. I had plenty at that time and had I allowed it, it could have caused me to make the choice to "stay for stuff." But after prayerfully weighing everything, I'm clear that the decision I made was best for me. Making the decision to walk away was an extremely difficult decision to make. My friend, I shared the material blessings I'd acquired in marriage not to brag, but instead to show the truth of the fact that materials don't always bring true joy and happiness. And yes, there have been some tough days in adjusting to being single, but through it all, God has been with me providing, loving me, keeping me, guiding me, protecting and strengthening me every step of the way. I wouldn't trade the peace of mind I have today for anything! This is no judgment on anyone else who decides to remain in a toxic situation. Everyone must make the decision that's best for them. I realized that my situation was not God's best for me. I also realized that dimming my light for the sake of someone else's insecurities was not how I wanted to live the rest of my life. I knew that living a life of wondering who was smiling in my face, but also stabbing me in my back, was not the life for me. Please understand that I'm not speaking as an advocate for divorce, I'm simply stating what was best for me. I'm simply sharing my story in hopes of encouraging someone else that you don't have to remain in this or any type of toxic relationship. Although I made the mistake of making an important lifelong decision without inviting God to be a part of it from the very beginning, my prayer is that you won't make the same mistake. I want my children and all who may be reading to know how important it is to include God in every decision. Yes, it is true that with every decision comes a consequence, but I also know that if there is true repentance, God forgives bad decisions and will give you the grace to endure and overcome consequences from those bad decisions! I am a living witness that God not only extends mercy and grace, but He will also use bad decisions to teach us some things we need to know about ourselves. You see my friend, with all the good that came from my marriage it still ended. It was important for me to focus on my responsibility in why my marriage ended by looking at the bigger picture. Although God chose to bless my marriage despite some mistakes, that does NOT negate the importance of consulting God from the very beginning when choosing a lifelong partner. It's imperative to do so! Building a solid foundation is critical when planning to spend the rest of your life with someone. Two people being Christians ONLY does not guarantee a successful marriage. Being "an ideal cute couple" only, is not a good recipe for a successful marriage. I've learned how important it is to be on the same page in every way when choosing a partner for life. It's important to take the time finding out if the two of you REALLY fit.

What God doesn't join together is subject to be put asunder. When there are issues in marriage sometimes the two parties involved tend to spend a lot of time pointing fingers of blame towards one another. But I've found that there are times in marriage when your foundation is tested. More importantly than pointing fingers is examining the foundation of your relationship. You see my friend, with all of the hurt that occurred, I realized we had simply hit some hurdles that were too enormous for us to conquer and recover from. The question then became, "Why were those hurdles too enormous for us to cross together"? Although uncomfortable, sometimes the tough questions must be asked and answered. The tough question in my situation being, although God's grace was poured upon us "Did God join us together"? There may be some who stood at the altar and made commitments to God and another person in public, but without including Him in the choosing process in private. I can only speak for myself when I say I didn't consult God when getting married. No, this is not something I'm proud of. You see, It's not always easy to face your truth my friend, but a certain freedom and peace comes when you do. After 19 years, my marriage ended in divorce. At first, I had trouble understanding how and why this happened. We'd helped so many through their marriages and those people are still together today. I kept thinking, "where did it go wrong"? How could someone I've known for many years, lived under the same roof with, slept in the same bed with, share children with become someone I could no longer live in harmony with? You see, understanding the cause of my marital breakdown became more important than pointing out flaws, mistakes or who did what to whom. I heard a dear friend once say, "Sometimes in life, you must peel back the layers in order to get to the root of a problem." I found this statement to be absolutely true.

Understanding is always found when going back to the foundation of a matter. As I began peeling back layers in my own life it helped explain just how a marriage of many years, that produces beautiful children can STILL end. When the love that had grown faded and the trust was destroyed, sadly we had nothing to hold us together. Peeling back layers by going back to the beginning has helped me discover where the weaknesses originated in my marriage. I saw clearly that the foundation of my marriage was weak. And with anything if the foundation is weak, it will soon crumble.

Because of the pain and bizarre events that took place in my marriage, I've often said with conviction that I'll never get married again, but honestly only God knows my future. I've even gotten specific by stating, "I'll never marry a Pastor again." I must be honest and say that initially my painful experiences did put a bitter taste in my mouth towards marriage, pastors, and church to the point where I wanted no parts of either. It was devastating to experience that level of pain and never receive an apology. It was heartbreaking to experience how, when it became evident that I'd made the choice to walk away, some church members I'd once considered family, chose to turn their backs on me and continue following their pastor no matter what had been done. That was a very painful experience. It was mind blowing to experience how he, instead of choosing to step down as Pastor, chose to silence me instead. I could never understand that and still don't to this day. Yes, those were painful experiences, but after some time, and much prayer I've given those things to God. I realize that no one is perfect, and we all have to answer for our own actions in life. Although some of my experiences in being married to a pastor were unpleasant and painful, I recognize that does not make all pastors bad or all men bad. I certainly don't have a vendetta against Pastors and churches, I come from a family of ministers and Pastors. I am simply sharing some of my hurtful experiences in life and how I've overcome those painful events with God's help. Getting through my pain was very instrumental in developing this mindset.

God knows my future and one thing for sure is that whatever future decisions I make; those decisions certainly won't be made without God's input from the very start. Through life's circumstances we learn what to do and what not to do. Oftentimes, people get married for all the wrong reasons instead of prayerfully considering and carefully examining the whole person and situation. My friend, my advice to you is that you'd use proper insight when choosing a lifelong mate. Don't base your decision on childish insignificant things like whether you're a "cute couple," who you might make cute babies with or the fuzzy feelings you may have in the beginning of your relationship. Base your decision on whether your heart truly connects with his or hers? It's important that you're both connected spiritually. It's important to become friends first. Base your decision on whether your goals and dreams work together. To know the answer to these questions, that person must be prayerfully observed. When you ask yourself the question of whether the two of you fit, do it without any thoughts of fixing or overlooking anything in your mind. If there are places where the two of you don't quite gel in the beginning, don't overlook that my friend. Instead, heed to small signs that will become larger later. Base your decision on honesty with yourself first.

My friend I will admit to you that going through divorce is a very difficult process especially when there are children involved. Going through divorce can make you feel like a failure. Although my father was not in favor of my decision to get married, when my marriage came to an end he never said, "I told you so". He was loving, supportive in many ways and always told me that me and my children would be ok. Even when my mind said, go back and give it another chance, my father simply said to me, "I don't think God delivered you from Egypt to go back to Egypt." That advice helped me greatly during a time when my emotions had gotten cloudy. Although my marriage ended in a painful divorce, I thank God all was not lost! I'm grateful for the good times and bad times. I'm grateful for every blessing God afforded me while being married. Along with being thankful for the many lessons learned, I'm most grateful for being blessed with three beautiful children who are now all adults! I consider the opportunity of being their mother to be my GREATEST accomplishment. Throughout my marital breakdown I was constantly concerned and praying about my children. They were all hurting in their own way. And being their mother, I wanted to fix it and take all their pain away but sadly I couldn't. Not being able to fix it and take their pain away grieved my heart. But I turned to the one who could ease their pain. Today I'm so thankful to God for bringing them through the pain they've experienced from the divorce, and I pray daily for any painful residue to be removed from their hearts. They could have used their pain from the divorce as a reason to give up, but instead with Gods help they chose to press through their pain. And as a result, they are all adults who have not turned their backs on God. They have all persevered through their pain and recently I watched my baby girl walk across the stage to receive her bachelor's degree! I'm now the proud mother of three college graduates! Glory to God! They have their struggles as we all do, but they are learning to trust God through them all!

I'm grateful for the beautiful times and many years of grace God afforded me during my marriage. It was through my marriage where God afforded me the opportunity to meet and positively touch the lives of many people and to also be touched by some beautiful souls as well and for that I'm grateful. After grieving over the death of my marriage, God reminded me that although the marriage ended, His purpose for me didn't end! His purposes remain the same! My pain did not forfeit my purpose! I'm thankful that through the marital pain I've experienced, my trust and faith in Him have been strengthened! Today I'm grateful for the pain. The pain didn't feel good at all, but I kept waking up every morning, putting one foot in front of the other and persevering through it! Although my children knew what had transpired with their father, I never spoke negatively about him to them. My focus remained on getting us through the pain as best I could. I didn't allow the pain to make me hateful or bitter. As painful as that time in my life was, God STILL brought some GOOD out of that pain. I'm stronger and wiser today! I'm thankful to God for maturing me in areas where He knew I needed growth. Overall, I'm thankful to God for giving me the mind and strength to endure the pain and making me BETTER and not become bitter through the pain!

Chapter 5

THE PAIN OF BETRAYAL

So many have loosely used the quote, "I got your back," but really have no clue of what that truly means. I've had some "I got your back" folk in my life. But I've also experienced being backstabbed by some of the same folk who once said they had my back. Have you ever trusted someone with your most precious gifts? She was my assistant. Our boys were best friends. We shopped together and took road trips together. I trusted her in my home. I trusted her in my former husband's company when I wasn't around. She babysat my children when I needed to make trips out of town to visit my mother who was ill at the time. One of the last visions I saw of her in my home was a time when she was giving my daughter a bath. She was a person that constantly told me, "I got your back"! As time went on, she began changing her appearance in attempts to mirror me.

There is a quote that was first coined by Charles Caleb Colton which states, "Imitation is the sincerest form of flattery." I must admit and disagree, there was nothing flattering about her attempt to imitate me. In fact, her attempts to imitate me were more irritating than flattering. She added hair attempting to copy my hairstyles. She bought glasses mirroring mine. She began attempting to dress like me. In some cases, even wearing clothing I had given her. As things became even more strange, it then became noticeably clear by her actions that she was coveting my entire life. She took "admiration" to a whole new and sick level. My friend, she was attempting to be me, not realizing that she could never be me. You see, anyone can attempt to duplicate your "look", but what one can never accomplish is duplicating another's essence. Her actions proved that she was oblivious to the fact that there is only one Freshun Eleana Wilson and could never be another. Please don't judge me my friend. I say that not out of arrogance, but instead out of Godly confidence! When God created me, He broke the mold! Don't you feel the same way about yourself? If not, you should my friend. You are one of a kind! Don't ever forget that. He's too creative to make duplications of His creations. The purpose God has for your life is only for you. And no matter how the enemy attempts to harm you, or duplicate you, or take what only belongs to you, it won't work! Understand my friend that even when we are unaware of all that is going on around us God is aware of it all and working on our behalf to protect us. Although hurtful at the time, I am thankful to God for showing me during one of my worst times, who really had my back and who did not.

After rumors began to surface, I'd ask him if the rumors were true, and the answer would always be a very stern" no"! He followed it by reprimanding me for listening to the "wrong people". But finally, after much pressure, by his admission I was told it was true. He admitted to me with anger," yes, I did it and now you can't hold it over my head." What a mind-boggling response I thought. Those words rang in my head for many years. By his admission and then later hers, they both admitted to me that they were guilty. During our separate conversations she blamed him, and he blamed her. This pain of betrayal stemming from not one, but two sources simultaneously, is enough to cause major damage to both the betrayed and the betrayer. Not only was hearing that the rumors were true painful, but also experiencing the great lengths in which he traveled to try and prove none of them were true. The constant lies and reprimands were troubling. They caused me to question my relationship with God and others who had my best interest at heart. Having a meeting in our home with elders and deacons of the church for the purpose of removing "her" from the church was unreal to say the least. As I sat next to him in support, he continued portraying her as the "loose, trouble-making woman" at the church, and the elder acted accordingly. When the truth of the matter was he'd made the huge mistake of being involved with that "loose woman." My friend, I understand how the pain of betrayal can leave deep wounds and visible scars. I'm extremely thankful to God for allowing me to still have my right mind because when your trust has been violated it causes great trauma within you. Being in a relationship whether friendship, marriage, or family you naturally believe that they will never hurt you. Emotions from betrayal can range from shock, anger, insecurity, and rage to humiliation, loneliness, confusion, shame, and grief. And believe me, I've experienced them all and more. But again, I'm grateful to God for bringing me through that devastating time in my life. Again, I want you to know that I'm sharing some of my personal experiences to simply let you know that you are not alone when it comes to experiencing pain in this life.

I'm very thankful to God that although I did destroy some materials, He restrained me from causing bodily harm to anyone during that time. Trust me my friend, it didn't feel good finding out after months and months of speculation that some rumors alleged in the" letters" were INDEED true. During that time, I had gotten very angry with some in defense of him. Then it was later revealed to me that their anger with him was in defense of me. You see, these people had gotten wind of the inappropriate behavior and were not happy with him because of it. I guess I'd heard the phrase "the devil is attacking" so much I had taken on the posture of believing it by "standing by my man". As you can imagine, I was devastated! I felt like a fool. At that moment I hated him. I think I had temporarily lost my mind. I had begun beating myself up. I felt as if I was the last to know the truth. Looking back, I could see where I'd missed some signs. While grieving over this situation, I beat myself up repeatedly. I was so busy taking care of my family and helping to build his dreams I did not realize that our children being best friends with hers at the time was actually all a cover-up. I couldn't see that she was coveting my life. At that moment, the reason behind her sick obsession to duplicate me became clear. So many questions circled in my head like, "Why did he allow her to hurt me." He was in charge of everything and had the final approval on who my assistants would be, but never said a word. I could not seem to understand how her conscience allowed her to comfortably be in my world knowing what had transpired. She smiled in my face and assisted me wholeheartedly it seemed, but behind the smile was a hidden agenda. Even then God was totally ware of the hidden agenda.

As hurtful as it was at the time, my relationship with God is what strengthened me enough to trust that He would somehow heal my heart, mind, and spirit. Today, I'm thankful to be able to say that He has. I won't pretend as though I never experience thoughts of "the betrayal," however the thoughts no longer send me to a dark mental place, instead they send me to a thankful place! If a thought from that time enters my mind it no longer causes me anger and hurt to the point of wanting revenge. That's major growth for me and I'm thankful for it. Just another example of how God will work a harmful situation out for your good! I'm a firm believer that God has ALL power, so I've had times of wondering why God allowed me to find out the truth after years of not knowing. I asked God one day, "Lord, why didn't you keep this covered?" They had gotten away with it until God led me to remove some assistants. That's when things began to rumble. When I asked God why He'd allowed this to happen, He answered me by simply saying, "Because I love you, and I didn't want you to be unaware." I didn't quite understand it then, but God was preventing me from spending any further time with the enemy. You see my friend; God loves us so much that He'll expose what's harmful to us not to hurt us but for our good. He delivered me from unknowingly allowing my enemy in my home. He delivered me from unknowingly giving my enemy free access to my family. It was all a part of His plan! God truly DOES have our backs. He knows what we need, how and when we need it even before we ask for help. And what does He require in return? He simply requires our trust. My friend, although painful, God loves us too much to allow us to be unaware of enemies in our lives who may be causing us harm. I understand how heartbreaking it is to find out that someone who claims to "Have your back" is really stabbing you in the back. But I'm thankful that GOD really did have my back! Although I was unaware of the truth, God knew it wasn't true when she would say it. Therefore, He exposed the situation. You see, even when we are unaware, we serve a God who is All Knowing and because He loves us, He will reveal those who are being used by the enemy to harm us! He did that for me and I'm grateful! So remember, God has your back no matter what.

I could have chosen to harbor bitterness in my heart towards them both, but today I'm glad that I didn't. In the end what good would that have done for me? Absolutely none. I realized that hating those who have harmed me is not worth my inner peace. Therefore, I chose to let it all go, focus on moving forward, and watch God do the rest. I found that meditating on revenge only keeps you stuck in the past. Rehearsing the offense in your mind only keeps you in a mental prison. My strong desire to move forward caused me to do whatever was necessary to do so. Over time I realized how important the act of forgiveness was for me! I got to a place where I desperately wanted to move forward, and my friend, forgiveness helps you do that. Never underestimate the importance of forgiveness. I realized that this is something that needed to be done for me, whether I ever received an apology or not. I needed to be ok. I needed to move on. I needed peace inside. I also thought about the times God has forgiven me repeatedly, so there was no way I could not forgive my enemies. Now please understand me when I say, when you forgive someone, that does not necessarily mean you want to sit and have lunch with your enemy. Well, at least it did not happen that way for me. Forgiving someone does not mean that you forget the hurtful acts. It means that you choose to live in spite of the hurtful acts. My friend, keep in mind that forgiveness is for you! Forgiveness gives you freedom! Forgiveness gives you a sense of inner strength! Forgiveness has many health benefits! Forgiveness helps you heal. Forgiveness reduces your stress and anxiety. Forgiveness gives you mental peace. Forgiveness gives you your power back. That alone is enough for me to choose forgiveness over getting revenge. My friend, when you choose to forgive, you are simply choosing to let go of the painful past and focus on moving forward. There is power in forgiveness. I understand that there are times when you may have to forgive without an apology. But I encourage you to be strong enough to forgive them even without an apology.

Remember, forgiveness benefits you, not the offender. Getting to this place was not easy for me. There was a time when I would meditate on ways to get revenge, but then I was reminded that vengeance does not belong to me it belongs to God. There was a time when I didn't think I would make it through the excruciating pain of betrayal, but day by day God has healed my heart and mind. God has carried me through it all. Today I am thankful that instead of getting revenge, I trusted God to strengthen me through the pain and ease the pain. I trusted God to help me forgive. Although it did not happen overnight, the important thing is that over time it did happen. God eased my pain and strengthened my heart. He helped me get over the desire to get revenge and I am grateful he did. He then gave me the strength to forgive those who had harmed me. If you are struggling with forgiving those who have caused you harm, God is there able and willing to strengthen you wherever you are experiencing weakness in your heart. Continue turning to Him and continue to trust Him.

You see my friend; God is the one person we can trust to truly have our backs in life. Remember, God's got you! He's trustworthy! He's dependable! He won't tell your secrets! He gives great advice, and He loves unconditionally! And my friend, God won't betray your trust!

Chapter 6

PAIN OF A DEVASTATING DIAGNOSIS

As I stated before, 2007 was a very trying year. Amid my divorce proceedings 2007 was also the year I became extremely ill. This was the most frightening time of my life. I had moved to Chicago Il. It was a time I spent many days in emergency rooms and doctors' offices. It all started one extremely hot day while enjoying the pool with my children. I began feeling very weak with a strange tightening feeling around my abdomen. The next strange feeling happened some days later while I was working. I remember sitting at my desk feeling my arms and legs becoming very limp and weak. I had lost control of my extremities and it was a very frightening feeling. The next thing I recall is seeing my father standing in the emergency room with me. After a few tests they couldn't give me a solid answer as to what the problem was. Therefore, I left with possibilities of what it could be, but not knowing for sure why I was feeling ill. The next episode happened while driving on a busy expressway. Both my legs and feet became very weak which made it difficult to accelerate or break. It was only by the grace of God that I was able to coast until slowing down to pull over safely. At that point I was overtaken with fear and did what came naturally which was to call my mother.

During that time, although she was struggling with her own health issues, she gave me what I needed at the time, which was her comfort, and assurance that I was not alone and that I would be ok. I was then taken to another hospital only to be told the same as before, that I was possibly experiencing something called neuropathy. Shortly thereafter, the weakness started again, only this time, it was a bit worse than before and lasted longer. The only way to describe what I was feeling is to describe it as my body feeling heavy, like lead. I recall on this day not being able to lift myself from the bathtub. I called my sister who happened to live 45 min away, but that didn't matter. When she arrived, she didn't ask a lot of questions, but instead helped me get dressed and swiftly drove me to get the help I desperately needed. We were sent from one facility to another trying to get answers to the underlying cause of why I wasn't feeling well. I recall as we sat in the emergency room of another hospital, being asked to sign my name, but I couldn't. I recall looking at my sister and daughter when this happened. Although my sister tried to keep her cool, I could see the worry in her eyes. She was my rock throughout this process. My daughter was young and never cried, but was concerned and observant to what was occurring. After many weeks of hospital visits, several nerve tests and MRI's, I was finally hospitalized and diagnosed with Multiple Sclerosis. I was both shocked and devastated by the diagnosis.

Multiple Sclerosis also known as MS is a POTENTIALLY disabling disease of the brain and spinal cord (central nervous system). MS blocks messages between the brain and the body. MS also causes the immune system to attack itself. When first diagnosed, I went through a period of denial, self-pity, depression and even shame. Finding out I had MS was both shocking and very shattering to me. I didn't know much about the disease at that time. The only people I knew who had struggled with the condition were Richard Pryor and a friend of my mother. Both cases ended in long strenuous battles with the disease then death. I thought about my mother's friend and how beautiful she was. I reflected on the terrible toll the disease had taken on her body. This woman had once been so vibrant, such a sharp dresser and beautifully built. She wore the best of everything. She was a woman who was beautiful both inside and outside and was so full of life. But after a few years of having the disease, she turned into a totally different person physically. She lost her eyesight and lost her ability to walk on her own and take care of herself. Her husband took care of her until her death. It was a very sad situation to witness. It was quite the same with Richard Pryor. We all knew him as being this cool witty guy with a sharp tongue and great sense of humor. But after suffering from this disease, towards the end of his life, he had almost turned into a vegetable. I thought about pictures I'd seen of him shortly before his death. The pictures showed him in a wheelchair and no longer able to walk or take care of himself. And as I thought about having the same disease, I was traumatized. I thought about my mother's sweet friend who had depended very highly on her husband's care later in her life. Then I thought about myself, being in the middle of divorce proceedings and wondering, "who will take care of me when I can no longer take care of myself"? It was a very scary thought. I shared those thoughts with my doctor, and he encouraged me to stay positive and NOT to focus on anyone else's case because all cases are different. He stressed the importance of remaining stress free. Knowing how stressful my divorce proceedings were at the time, hearing this sounded impossible which brought on much anxiety. After being diagnosed there were some who struggled with my diagnosis to the point of skepticism. Although this was painful to experience, I can somewhat understand because the disease is very unpredictable and not easy to comprehend. You see, one day you can be fine and look like a picture of good health, and the next day can be the total opposite. I'm not certain, but perhaps this is what caused their skepticism. Nevertheless, what I knew I couldn't and wouldn't do was be worried about who believed me or not. Multiple Sclerosis is a very strange condition to carry, and the uncertainty of it all can be frustrating and mentally exhausting which can lead to extreme fatigue and depression if not careful. Therefore, my focus had to be on remaining stress free in order to live a healthy life. After a week in the hospital, I was sent home with discharge instructions which included having to inject myself every other day with medication. I HATE needles with a passion and hearing this brought on more fear and depression. But again, I had to do what I had to do in order to live. This is when I turned inward and began to trust in the Lord with all my heart. God was all I could rely on. I knew that only HE could help me remain stress free while adjusting to carrying such a stressful and uncertain condition inside my body in the midst of hostile divorce proceedings.

I've often wondered why I felt a sense of shame when first being diagnosed with MS. Sometimes when going through struggles in life, without realizing it we can begin feeling sorry for ourselves. I do know that although I may have pitied myself at that time, I never wanted to be the subject of negative conversation or to be looked upon with pity. Many times, people who live with illnesses are looked upon as weak. I struggled with that because although I was weak, I didn't want to appear weak. I felt a sense of shame because being their mother, I was supposed to be strong for my children. But no matter how I tried to toughen up for them and for myself, at that time in my life I was very weak. There were even times I hid when injecting myself simply because I didn't want my children to see me weak or struggling with an illness. This brought on feelings of shame and pity. My emotions were everywhere at that time, however I'm thankful that with God's help over the years I've grown and matured. Experiencing pain will cause you to grow up. Some things that once bothered me no longer do. The feelings of shame I once carried about the condition are no longer there. It no longer matters to me what people think or say. It is what it is as they say. I realize the condition I carry does NOT define who I am. Yes, I have the condition, but the condition does NOT have me! With or without the condition I am who I am. Instead of feeling sorry for myself, I consider it a privilege and honor that God would entrust me to carry such a serious condition. He knew that no matter how difficult the condition was to carry; I would get through it. No matter how much daily pain I'd endure or how many fearful tears I would cry, how many lonely MRI's I'd endure, no matter how rough the relapses, how painful the self-injections were, how many lab tests, or how many lengthy steroid infusions I'd have to endure, although I didn't recognize the strength I had inside, He was with me and knew that I would NEVER give up and turn my back on Him!

As I worked through this process, I experienced God's strength and love firsthand. This situation has strengthened my trust in God. My faith has been fueled. It encouraged me to lean and totally depend on Him and I encourage you to do the same through your process. This situation confirmed to me that I am in control of nothing, but that God is in control of everything! These firsthand experiences have drawn me closer to Him. He doesn't have to prove himself to anyone, but He chose to prove Himself to me and continues to do so today. And my friend He doesn't love me any more than He loves you. Whatever your challenges in life may be, keep trusting in God, believing in yourself and keep walking until you get to the other side of your pain. It's been 14 years since the diagnosis and with some trying challenges along the way, God continues to show Himself strong in my life! I recognize that with every struggle I may endure brings a new testimony! Therefore, I've chosen to trust God in this and every situation. Although MS is a potentially disabling disease, I focus on the word POTENTIALLY. My trust is NOT in what the disease can or will do, my trust is in GOD and His power that keeps me. I trust in the one who is in control of the disease. There was a time when fear about the disease would overtake me. Having to endure MRI's and tests alone was both frightening and depressing. But as I began truly trusting God with my life and the disease, I realized that I don't have to be afraid of the disease. God is bigger than MS and any other condition!

Through every painful and frightening situation related to this condition, I'm able to trust Him more today, because I'm well aware of what He's done for me many times before. When first diagnosed, during the period of feeling sorry for myself, I had questions for God. I asked Him,

``Why are you allowing me to go through this alone"? I often wondered why God didn't allow me to experience this diagnosis while married. But I recognize that going through this alone has taught me to trust and have faith in God alone. The painful events that have transpired have also equipped me to encourage you to hang in there and keep going my friend. You can do this!

Chapter 7
PAIN GIVES CLARITY

I've known for a very long time that I was being led to share my story but didn't quite know how. I started journaling while going through problems in my marriage. Those journals consisted of everything I was going through and feeling at the time of writing. God later, although He didn't give all the specifics, placed in my spirit that a book would come from the painful events in my life. Authoring a book was the furthest thing from my mind when I began writing. Over the years some circumstances and events in my life caused me to pause in writing. With all the changes I couldn't quite figure out how to put it all together or how to make it make sense for others. At times those pauses turned into complete stops as I would try convincing myself that it wasn't God's will for me to author a book. But it never failed every time I took a break or stopped; God would push me right back to writing. I struggled for a few years with how to go about sharing my story. I never wanted to come off as a bitter woman because that's not who I am. Therefore, fear, others' opinions, and feelings of inadequacy caused me to shrink back. But the time came when those things no longer mattered. I realized that the most important relationship I have is my relationship with God. Those who would be helped by my testimony took precedence over everyone and everything else. And even more importantly than that, giving God all the glory that He's so deserving of became my goal. My friend, remember the enemy will always throw something in your path to try and keep you from fulfilling your purpose. I tried many times putting my goal of finishing this book on the back burner and acting as though I was ok with not writing and sharing my story, but the more I pretended to be ok, the more uncomfortable and restless I became. I allowed situations such as the death of my parents and lack of finances to cause me to turn my back on this project. Then of course the enemy had a field day with trying to convince me that I wasn't hearing from God, but during those times I would clearly hear God softly but firmly say," **KEEP WRITING." Therefore, I kept writing**. I'm thankful that God loved enough that He wouldn't allow me to be comfortable in my decision to quit. He's a good God Therefore He didn't badger me. But in His own sweet way He just wouldn't allow me to rest. I felt as though I was letting God down by keeping silent and not sharing about His goodness to me. Therefore, I kept writing! I had a longing to share my story for the purpose of helping someone else by pointing them to the God who has brought me through all my struggles. When you think about it, isn't that what we were all created to do? How else will God get His glory?

I recall one afternoon having a dreadful day. Everything was going wrong. While trying to get over not one but two MS relapses, I was diagnosed with yet another condition that affects my spine and could cause permanent paralysis. All of this occurred in 2020 during the coronavirus pandemic. Then along with these issues, I also endured major financial hardship. The most recent health condition I had been diagnosed with was causing me so much pain at that time. To ease the pain, my doctor scheduled an epidural shot to be taken through my neck. As painful and uncomfortable as that procedure was, after two weeks my pain was the same. The only option left to relieve my daily pain was orthopedic surgery which to this day I still have not undergone.

The next day I found myself feeling very overwhelmed. I woke up with thoughts about my finances and lack thereof, my health and did I forget to include my car issues. Oh yes, while all of this occurred my car's transmission died. Shortly after that I began having stabbing pains on my left side. I went to the ER and found out I had Pneumonia. My friend, ongoing pain and suffering is hard. Another thing I realized about pain and suffering is that it tends to cause you to isolate yourself from others. You see, I was suffering so much it became embarrassing. I was sick of being sick! It seemed that whenever I spoke with family or friends, I was suffering in some way. I knew I was not a hypochondriac and was not a fan of revealing my weaknesses. I was over it all! I was frustrated! I was suffering with pain from two conditions simultaneously! I was having one of those, "when it rains it pours" moments. All I could do was cry and that's ok. Someone once told me that crying cleanses the soul and I did plenty of it. I didn't want to talk to anyone. There were times when my family and friends would call, or text and I wouldn't respond. I'm not sure why, I just know I was feeling a way. I was so consumed with my struggles; I had begun to isolate myself from others without realizing it. I didn't want to reveal my struggles and weaknesses. I was simply tired of suffering. On top of what was happening in our country, I was worn out from the strain of constant struggles. With the country being semi shut down, there was a lot of time to scroll social media. When scrolling and looking at everyone living their "best life" it made my situation even more depressing. I wanted to be in a season of "Living my best life" also, but instead I was in a season where I was weak and dealing with some personal struggles. As I continued turning to God, He comforted me through His word and others. During the time I needed comfort, a listening ear, financial help, assistance during my illness, God had placed those special people in my life at the right time. That's when I was reminded that God receives glory when we don't act like we have it all together, but instead lean on Him and admit that almighty God is holding us together. I didn't understand that then, but I certainly do now. You see my friend, unlike social media, real life doesn't come with a filter. People only show their best pictures on social media. But no matter how perfect a life seems on social media, NO ONE lives a perfect, problem free life. God reminded me that we will ALL suffer in this life. Even the ones who are daily living out their "best lives" on social media.

After having a little breakdown, God led me to read some things I had recently written. As I began reading, I noticed that every word I had written was encouragement to me at that very moment. Little did I know that just by reading my OWN book I would be encouraged to keep going! I was not only encouraged to keep going, but also to **KEEP WRITING!** It dawned on me that if my own words helped me, then surely someone else would be helped and encouraged also. That's when it became clear to me that the pain we may endure in life is never for us, but instead it's to help someone else. I kept writing to encourage you to keep going my friend!

In scripture the Apostle Paul didn't plead once with God, but THREE times to remove his "thorn in the flesh." Like Paul there have been times in my life when I wanted God to take ALL my pain away. And although He didn't take it all away at that time, what He did do was give me the strength to endure and persevere through the pain. He showed Himself strong when I was weak! You see, Pain helps us discover God's power in weakness. Yes, my friends, I understand how pain and suffering can make you weak to the point of wanting to give up, but DON'T GIVE UP! You are not alone my friend.

At the very moment my trials had overwhelmed me, God's grace strengthened me to keep going! During that time God's encouragement to me in Isaiah 41:10 (NIV) became another favorite scripture where He says, ***"So do not fear, for I am with you; be not dismayed for I am your God. I will strengthen you and help you; I will uphold you with my righteous right hand."***

Remember God is there to help us. We have God's grace and it's sufficient which means it's enough for us ALL! Therefore, during your times of weakness remember that God's grace will empower you to do things you can't naturally do! His grace is sufficient for all who will acknowledge they need Him. Just Trust Him and lean into His help my friend. Recognize you are not alone! The devil THOUGHT he had shut me down, through marital trauma, and through a POTENTIALLY disabling condition, but GOD SAID NO!! I continued to trust Him through it all and I'm glad I did! I encourage you my friend, to give God a chance to show Himself STRONG in your life. I'm a living witness that if given the chance, He will!

Chapter 8

PAIN EQUIPS US TO HELP OTHERS

When pain takes its course it's no longer about you and me, but instead it's about the purpose for which we were predestined. It was strange that at the very same time I was dealing with my own issues, I had some friends who were also suffering physically and financially and friends who were losing loved ones. I found myself constantly checking on my friends and praying with them through their struggles. I was a listening ear when they needed to vent or cry, and always ended our conversations or texts saying, God is in control. I would pray for them in my own prayer time, and they would pray for me. My heart went out to them even during my own suffering. You see, even in my struggle I found myself able to encourage them from my own experiences with God as a provider, a comforter and healer. I didn't realize it then; I was just simply doing what I thought came naturally. But later after reading 2 Corinthians 1:3,4(NIV) which states, ***"Praise be to God the Father of our Lord Jesus Christ, the Father of compassion and the God of all comfort, who comforts us in ALL our troubles, so that we can comfort those in ANY trouble with the comfort we ourselves receive from God"***, I realized it was my higher power the Holy Spirit leading me to comfort others.

This word was very enlightening to me. It taught me that the storms we're in right now, coming out of, or going into, are not just for us, but instead they are for someone else. This is another reason we shouldn't attempt to avoid our storms and pain. Instead, our prayer as a believer should be, "Lord, give me the faith, strength and courage to face my storm so that I may be a help to others in their time of suffering". It's not God's plan for us to waddle and whine through our seasons of suffering. It's not His will for us to keep our struggles and weaknesses hidden and focus only on ourselves. God comforts us so that we may comfort others! God grants us mercy so that we can be merciful to others! God stands with us in our suffering so that we will stand with others in their suffering! Since losing my parents, I've had some friends lose parents and loved ones. And just as many have been there to comfort me, I've also been there to comfort others during their suffering. God never leaves us alone in our suffering so that we won't leave others alone in theirs! We are encouraged in ***Psalm 34:19 (NKJV)*** which states, ***"Many are the afflictions of the righteous, but God delivers him out of them all."*** There is no affliction that God is unaware of. There is no affliction that God is too distant from. God is interested in the care and comfort of his children in ALL our afflictions. I am a quiet and private person by nature.

Therefore, when going through trials and suffering, it's easy for me to isolate myself, turn inward and not want to be bothered. However, I've learned that it's not God's plan for us to suffer alone. When we suffer, we need to be comforted by someone who understands our pain. And God will always send who we need at just the right time. I recall how I felt when I'd lost my parents. I didn't want anyone who hadn't lost a loved one to tell me they knew how I felt or that it would get better. How would they know how I was feeling unless they'd experienced or gotten through the same pain? Who can better comfort you at a time of grief than someone who's experienced the loss of a loved one? When I lost my parents there were people who still had both parents who told me that the pain would ease up. While I appreciated their attempts to comfort me, and no disrespect to anyone, but honestly only a person who had been through the pain of losing a parent could tell me that it would get better. Only a widow can truly comfort the heart of another grieving widow. God is loving and caring, and part of His design for us when we suffer is to comfort us through other sufferers who have been through what we are facing. During those devastating times of losing my parents, there were many who were there to comfort me and my family. And I'm so thankful for the times I've experienced God's comfort through others. I'm also thankful for the opportunities He's given me to comfort others during their times of suffering.

Times when I've gotten quiet during my personal suffering, God has blessed me with family and friends who have checked on me and encouraged me whether I responded right away or not. They followed God's prompting to simply put a smile on my face and for that I'm eternally grateful. My father used to sing a song entitled, "No man is an island" written by Peter Schickele.

The words are: ***No man is an island, no man stands alone, each man's joy is joy to me, each man's grief is my own, we need one another, So I will defend, Each man as my brother, each man as my friend.***

As I've walked my personal journey, I've found these words to be true. Whether we choose to acknowledge it or not, we need one another. God wants us to know we're not alone which is why He sends people and supplies resources that help comfort, guide, strengthen, and encourage us in our times of suffering. Can you think of someone in your life who has been a help to you during a time of suffering? Someone who's given you an encouraging word or a random act of kindness. Maybe an encouraging text, or even a call to simply pray with you. Remember those times are not coincidences, but instead, comfort, care and concern from our Loving Heavenly Father working through others. God has everything we need in order to live our lives here on earth. In times of trouble, He may use others to help, encourage and comfort us, but what we must remember is that GOD is ultimately our source. When we rely on our own strength or the strength of others, it takes an opportunity from God to reveal His true power and love for us. Keep in mind, He will use you as a vessel to help someone else, or can use someone else to be a blessing to you in times of need. I'm so thankful to God for sending those in my life to be a help to me during my personal times of need. I'm thankful for all of those whom God has placed in my life to be a source of encouragement since my parents transitioned. And I'm equally thankful for the opportunities He has afforded me to help others in need. Needs are not always connected to money. There are sometimes in life when a simple smile, hug, or kind word can mean so much more than what money could ever buy. The key for us is to be open in allowing Him to reveal Himself as He sees fit. This my friend is why trusting God and having a close relationship with Him is so dire as we live our lives on earth. He's aware that we can't do it on our own. He's aware of our flaws and imperfections. He's also aware of His purposes in creating each of us. We need Him and He knows we need Him to help us carry out His purposes in our lives.

It's important to remember that one of the reasons God takes us through our storms is so that we can help someone in their storm. You see, God doesn't comfort us to simply make us comfortable, but instead so that we can comfort others during their time of need. I've learned that's how God works. God is strategic and places certain people in your life that will be a help to you in times of need. He blesses us with people that bring joy to our hearts and puts a smile on our faces during rough times. There are times in life when we can be guilty of overlooking blessings from God because it doesn't seem large enough. But I know how important it is to have someone in your life who simply makes you smile during times of sadness or struggle. I understand how important it is to have someone who believes in you even sometimes more than you believe in yourself. There are times in our lives when we will need a friend or family member who will simply say, "Keep going, everything will be okay" when we need it most. God blesses us with people in our lives who encourage us sometimes at our lowest moments. Do you have someone like this in your life? If you can say you have one good friend in this world, then you're blessed beyond measure. Those people are rare, should be treasured, and are gifts from God to us during times of difficulty.

Chapter 9

PAIN OF LOSING LOVED ONES

I may never totally understand why God took my mother at the age of 73 and my father at the age of 69. However, I am thankful that He healed them both. I'll be honest and say that I've questioned God as to why He allowed their suffering. Nevertheless, He took them from their suffering here on earth and for that I'm grateful! We must realize that when we ask God for healing, it may not always happen the way we want or expect it. I've learned that we must be open to His healing process. It's not a lack of faith if He decides to heal someone by taking them out of their misery as some may teach. What some may call "a lack of faith" is sometimes God's will. What helps me get through the pain of losing my parents is accepting God's will. His will was to heal them both by taking them home to be with Him. I realize it wasn't His will for them to remain here in misery. Although losing them was painful, it also brings me joy knowing by faith that they are free from their pain and sorrow. My mother will no longer suffer from the effects of two strokes. She will never have to sit another miserable day in a care facility. My mother had a relationship with God and was an extraordinarily strong woman. She was an immensely proud member of Alpha Kappa Alpha Sorority Inc. She was also an enormously proud member of the Top Ladies of Distinction Inc. She served as Supervisor of the Wood River District Youth Department, Southern Region for several years. My mother was a very sharp dressing woman and I've never seen any other woman wear a hat quite the way she could. In my opinion, when it came to dressing like a Queen, no one could hold a candle to my mother. She was an exceptionally beautiful woman and when entering a room her stunning beauty would turn the heads of everyone there. I learned from her how to be classy and sassy, but never trashy. She showed me that the essence of a lady comes from how she tastefully glows and not from bodily advertisements. My mother was a very elegant woman. She was also as hard working as she was elegant. She worked many years as a truant officer. And when times were tough, she even worked an overnight job to help ends meet. During her last days here on earth she struggled with some health challenges which later led to her needing a caretaker. I then became her caretaker and did my best in helping her keep her dignity while going through her aging process. When taking care of her became too strenuous for me alone, I was sadly forced to place her in a care facility. This was an extremely difficult decision to make because I always knew she would never be happy in a facility, but I had no other choice. My heart would break every day I visited her and would have to leave her there. She was my girl. Although some say parents should not be friends with their children, I take no shame in saying that my mother was my absolute best friend, and the respect line between us was NEVER crossed. My mother would not have tolerated that anyway.

My mother and I were remarkably close. I recall during some of our talks as a teenager, when counseling me she would say to me, "Girl, listen to me, I've been where you're TRYING to go". Then we would laugh. She had her way of making me feel comfortable enough to talk to her about anything. That close relationship carried over into my adult years. My mother had amazing wisdom. I witnessed her giving counsel to many other young women and wives over the years. Her counsel would sometimes come across humorous, but I've had many days of referring back to even her humorous wisdom. I learned how to be a strong woman by observing my mother. I learned how to carry myself with class and dignity by observing her. During my adult years whenever I faced fearful or painful times, she would encourage me by quoting her favorite scripture ***Joshua 1:9(NIV)*** which states, ***"Have I not commanded you? Be strong and courageous. Do not be afraid; do not be discouraged, for the Lord your God will be with you wherever you go."*** Out of all the things my mother instilled in me THIS one sticks with me the most. She left the word of God with me that strengthens me during times of hardship, fear, pain, or struggle. No matter what happens in life, I know God is with me.

My heart was broken when she went home to be with the Lord. It was during the time I had started my relocation to Atlanta Ga. Amid figuring out my move and exploring how and where to relocate her there with me, I would make twelve hour drives back and forth to tend to her. It was during that time when the Lord took her home to live with Him. She left in 2015 and I still have moments of sadness because she's no longer with me. I miss her terribly, but thinking about her being in the presence of God with no pain, or suffering is the only thing that brings me peace. She's with her heavenly Father and He can take care of her far better than I or any entire staff ever could. I'm thankful that I don't ever have to experience the pain of leaving her in a care facility. God knew her time here on earth was over. The day she went home to be with the Lord she was being serenaded with the peaceful sounds of an acoustic guitar. While listening to the music she peacefully slipped away. What a beautiful way to leave suffering on earth and walk into the presence of God. As painful as it was to lose her, God knew what was best for us both. I know she would not have been happy with me making twelve-hour trips up and down the highway. But God knew I would have continued to do what I could. I also knew living in a care facility was not what she desired. Therefore, God stepped in and made the decision that was best for us both. After she left, I reflected on some of our fun times together. I recall as she sat one day before she left, unexpectedly she smiled and said to me, "You tough Shun" (you're tough Shun)! Those were words she would use to express to someone how impressed she was with the way they looked or with what they had done. It was her Anita L. Wilson encouragement to someone like only she could give. It was something about the way she said it that would make anyone feel good about themselves and empower you to keep pushing. Today whenever I face trials I reflect on her words, and they encourage me to keep going no matter what!

Many days I have thoughts of my father no longer being here with me and it makes me sad. My father was my rock. My parents shared with me that it was my father who placed a stereo near her belly while pregnant with me so that I could hear music playing. Even then, they were forming me. It was my father who taught me to sing a song entitled, "I made a vow" at the tender age of 2 years old. After teaching me the song, one Sunday morning, he stood me up in a chair to sing that same song. I am who I am today musically because of his teaching and molding me. Being born a girl, I couldn't be his namesake, so he created the name "Freshun Eleana" so I could at least carry his initials. As a little girl I remember him calling me his "sidekick" because I traveled with him from church to church on Sundays as he performed his duties as musician in our city. I observed his musical mastermind at work as he taught and prepared many church choirs for Sunday worship services. It was during these observations where I learned the importance of being thorough when preparing a choir for worship. My father was also the chosen vocalist in our city for many church services, weddings and fashion shows. I took notice of how beautifully and powerfully he sang whether singing "You are the Sunshine of my Life" as a wedding vocalist, or "Peace be still" on a Sunday morning. I learned from him to always sing and teach with intensity, giving it your best and to always allow God to use me just as he did.

I couldn't help but think how much of a struggle his last days here on earth were. He had been diagnosed with Prostate cancer and lived several years after beating it, we thought. But the latter part of his life was an ongoing struggle with chemotherapy and radiation. He had been such a healthy and strong man most of his life. He was an anointed Pastor/Minister, and anointed singer/musician. He had pastored three churches in East St. Louis, Il., one of which he'd founded and organized. He had once managed a department store downtown East St. Louis Il. for many years and had employed many in our city. He had also been a member of the East St. Louis district #189 school board. My father had what's called "a heart of gold" and anyone who knew him would say the same. He was kind to everyone he came in contact with. It was very painful to witness how cruel cancer had been to him knowing how vibrant and full of energy he had previously been. In my opinion, he didn't deserve that. I'll admit I was a little upset with God for allowing his pain. My father was an extraordinary man, but was also very humble. I often asked God why my father had to suffer and why he had to die. I felt he had so much more life to live.

My worst fear about the disease began to manifest as I watched him quickly dwindle in his physical appearance. Not long before he went to be with the Lord, he endured major struggles adjusting to chemotherapy. It tore my heart apart to hear him through a phone call cry out "help me Lord" as he struggled. But just as I heard his cry, so did his heavenly father. The difference in God hearing him is that where I could only feel sorry and pray for him, God had the power to do something about my father's pain. It wasn't much longer after that; God answered his prayer. One morning my father quietly slipped away from his pain and suffering and entered the presence of the Lord. Although I felt that 69 was too young for him to go and that he had so much more life to live, God knew what was best. My heart was broken yet again when my father left to be with the Lord, but God knew what was best for him. I say again how can you argue with God's will when He is the one who knows what is best. I had to accept God's will so that I could receive His comfort. I took my father's death extremely hard! It was strange that although I am the oldest child, I felt like a lost little girl when he died. That may be difficult for some to understand. You see my father had always been there for me. He had given me both my first and second job. He was there for me and my children during the time of my divorce. He was pastoring a church in Chicago Il. at that time. It was then when he employed me with my third job as his administrative assistant and music director. As I stated before, my father was my rock! He had been there for me through all my rough, painful periods and struggles. He was even there for me and my siblings when our mother passed away. He was our strength! He was our leaning post! Therefore, losing him was very devastating for me. Other than God, I really had no one else to talk to about how deeply his death affected me. I struggled tremendously and even slipped into times of depression. My siblings and I are remarkably close and were there as much as possible for one another. We stayed in constant contact and still do. But they were also dealing with their individual pain. I felt as though my security blanket had been ripped from underneath me. I'm not sure if being divorced played a factor, nonetheless I took the death of my father extremely hard. Although I had acknowledged my father as being my rock, God proved HIMSELF to be my rock in the absence of my earthly father. It was during these times of intense pain where I learned how to lean and totally depend on God my Father!

Not very long before my father went to be with the Lord, He had begun not speaking very much. During that time, one of the beautiful things he spoke and left with us was, "His words are true." As he began to transition from earth to be with the Lord, although he was experiencing pain, it wasn't his pain he focused on, but instead at that moment he focused on the truth of God's word. I wish I knew exactly what caused him to say that, but if nothing else, what I do know is he had lived a full life at 69 years old. He was ending up his journey with God on this side. I can only imagine that in that moment his reflection over his life and walk with God caused him to utter "His words are true." I imagine as he reflected over his life, he could see places where God had kept him. I'm sure he could feel God's presence with him even during his pain. As I've continued to live, those words have been encouragement to me that God's word can be trusted. Those words have encouraged me to keep trusting in God no matter how painful my circumstances may be. I'm grateful for those words. I'm also grateful for the many songs my father taught me to sing even before I had experienced any tests or trials.

Although he's no longer with me he instilled some powerful words through songs and through the word of God that keeps me going daily. Now that I'm older and have experienced life I have a much better appreciation for all the beautiful nuggets both my father and mother left with me. With all the things my mother had endured on her journey, both difficulties as well as victories, it's comforting to reflect on some of her encouraging words to me during times of difficulty. I recall her one day saying to me unexpectedly, in her distinct Anita L. Wilson Voice "you gone be ALRIGHT Shun"! Translation: "You're going to be ALRIGHT Shun"! I remember her saying those words with a smile and look of pride, admiration, and confidence. At the time I didn't know why she said it, I just smiled and told her, "Thanks Mama." I've often wondered exactly what caused her to assure me that I would be ok. I'll never pretend to be so spiritual by saying that I know exactly why my mother uttered those words that day. And although I'll never truly know the answer to why, it is my belief that my mother trusted the same God that had taken care of her to also strengthen, provide, and take care of me along my journey. It's my belief that she knew I would have some fearful and painful days where I'd feel like giving up. I also believe she knew and trusted that the same God who had kept and protected her throughout her journey would also keep me throughout my journey. And she was right. From the time I was in her womb to this present moment God has kept me. He brought me through every mountain and valley. He's strengthened me through all my hardships and painful situations! He's protected me and provided for me in every season. He healed me and comforted me at times when I desperately needed Him!

My friend, I understand the feelings of holes in your heart when losing loved ones, and more specifically, losing both of your parents. Not to make anyone else's loss unimportant or less painful. My closest experience with death just happens to be the loss of my parents. These are the people who gave me life. My journey of accepting the fact that

I must go on living in this world without them has been a very painful reality to accept. I honestly feel that the only thing that will completely heal my heart is when I see them again. Until then, I trust that God will continue giving me the grace to go on living a full life without them. This is what they would both desire me to do. There've been times social media memories have popped up. Sometimes the pictures of my parents have shaken me to tears, and other times the memories have brought me joy. I've learned to allow myself to feel what I need to feel. I realize there is no perfect way to walk your journey or go through your process of grief after losing a loved one. Although losing loved ones is a normal part of life it doesn't take the pain away. Remember, it's ok to NOT be ok sometimes when you've lost a loved one. It's also ok to smile on your loved one's birthday instead of cry. And it's ok when you feel the periodic stabbing pains from the reality of their absence. Let the tears flow if needed and enjoy the joyful days! My friend, these experiences simply mean we're human having weak moments in life. Through difficulties, mountains, and valleys, smiles, and tears, remember that no matter where we are in life, God is with us through it all! Keep reminding yourself that there is a PURPOSE in it all! And because of that you, we all have something Good to look forward to if we continue to Trust Him! Although I miss my parents terribly, I'm so thankful to God for not allowing their suffering to continue. He loved them more than I ever could and decided to take them out of the misery. He healed and delivered them by taking them to be with Him. Although their absence here on earth is painful it has drawn me so much closer to God. Where I could once depend on my mother's encouragement and advice, or my father's help and guidance. I now depend totally on God's daily wisdom, guidance, help and strength! I will always honor my mother and father, but God knew I wouldn't always have them and wanted me to realize that HE is my rock! The more I've lived and experienced trials the deeper my dependence on GOD has become. And the more I depend on Him the more I experience His love for me. The more I experience His love for me the more I TRUST HIM. You see my friend; God knows what we need. It may not always feel good. It may be frightening, but never doubt. Always remember that God has a good plan for your life. Mistakes, circumstances, bad decisions, or even wrong moves will not forfeit His plan for us if we would only continue to trust Him. Remember He's an All-Knowing God and is not surprised by any events that may take place in our lives. God knew His purpose for creating me was for Him. Therefore, He loved me enough to take me through some things. He didn't allow these things for the purpose of hurting me, but instead to remind me that He was with me and to make me a better vessel for His glory.

Chapter 10

PAIN STRENGTHENS OUR DEPENDENCE ON GOD

I was born and raised in the great city of East St. Louis Il. Growing up as an only child for several years helped shape me. I don't recall wanting very much when I was a child. Although my birthday was the day after Christmas, my parents never used that as an excuse to hold back from showering me with gifts and love for both Christmas and birthday. They took exceptionally good care of me. I guess you could say I was a little spoiled. I wouldn't say I was a brat; I was simply the only child and had all my parents' attention as only children do. Even when my siblings Fredrick Jr. and Anita arrived on the scene, my parents never neglected one child for the other. They always did their best in making sure we were all taken care of and had the best they could provide. From private schools to living in a good neighborhood, they showed us that nothing was too good for their children. As the oldest child I never had to work very much because my father was there and able to give me employment opportunities.

When I got married, I had gone from my mother and fathers care to my former husband's care. Not long after marriage I did open a home beauty salon to help ends meet. Then later in my marriage, when our family began to grow, I became a stay-at-home mom and homemaker. Therefore, my career for almost 20 years was taking care of my family.

Getting married at such an early age and not having much work experience outside the home caused me to be very dependent on my former husband. I realized even well after divorce in certain ways I was still dependent on him. He had been the ultimate bread winner. While not having to work a 9-5 job outside of my home was a blessing, and many women would give anything to have that type of life, it also turned out to be somewhat of a handicap for me. By that, I simply mean it caused me to be very dependent on man. But God was aware of my entire story. He knew all of that when he chose me. And He wanted me to realize that HE was all I needed to depend on. I've often reflected on how ironic it was in 2002 that my brother would ask me to record a song on his CD project entitled "He knows what's best for me". The words that I sang in that song were almost prophetic of what was to come in my life. There are times in life when we won't know what's lurking around the corner, because our knowledge is limited. But God foreknew the joys and jolts I'd experience in life. Now I know it was not by accident or happenstance, but by divine intent that God allowed my brother to ask me to record that particular song. That song has encouraged me many days since recording it. God knew there were areas in my life where I needed maturing, because He knew what was to come in my life. Therefore, He allowed me to experience pain, suffering and struggle, then used those trials to mature me so that I could encourage others! He truly knew what was best for me! Now I'm able to sing that song and others not because of what I heard about God but instead from what I KNOW about Him. You see my friend; growth is not an automatic result of having trouble. While in the midst of difficulty, we must choose the right attitude and then refuse to give up! God loves us too much to only allow life's good times. As a flower needs both sun and rain to grow, so do we. Growth happens when we make up our minds to press through difficulty without giving up. I can see clearly now how He used my trials to build me up in places where I was weak. Through my trials I learned my strengths and my weaknesses. My relationship with God has become stronger through every painful and fearful struggle.

There were times after divorce when starting life all over became fearful. I walked away from a painful situation not alone, but with my three children. Because I had been financially dependent on my former husband, thoughts of losing child support and alimony would haunt me. I had depended on it for so long and throughout my marriage I had been made to feel as though I could not make it on my own. During times of contemplating walking away or staying I'd been told many times I'd have nothing without him if I walked away. I guess after being told something for so long you begin to believe it, and a part of me did. It was during my struggles alone where God revealed Himself as my provider. If not for the struggles I wouldn't know Him as well as I do. Therefore, I'm grateful for every past struggle and any struggles to come, because no matter how difficult I believe by faith that they will work out for my good!

There were those who had advised me to "stay for the children." But staying in a toxic relationship for my children's sake was not the answer for me. It was not only toxic for me, but it had also become toxic for them. They had all begun displaying signs of emotional distress. While I didn't want them coming from a broken home, neither did I want them living IN a broken home. For these reasons and others, I struggled with what decision was best. Yes, my friend, "to leave or to stay" was a very frightening decision to make. This had been my life. This had been my children's life. My life and welfare had been in his hands for almost 20 years. But with all those things and more taken into consideration, I took the huge frightful step of faith. No, it hasn't always been easy, but the peace of mind has been worth it all. I learned through this situation that God wanted me to know without a doubt that HE was my source, and HE was all I needed to depend on. God provided all I needed and became all I could depend on and not once has He allowed me to fail. I did not say there have not been rough periods. Since going through a major life change from the death of my marriage, the death of my parents, a health crisis and other challenges, God has been there with me through it all! After divorcing I was still able to lean on the strength of my parents. But after experiencing the devastating loss of them both, God has been there carrying me through it all! God has strengthened me through it all! He has brought me through it all! It has never been my intention to ignore Him. However, in looking back I see times when I panicked instead of truly trusting in God and leaving all consequences to Him. Panicking instead of trusting Him will sometimes cause you to make desperate decisions, and desperate decisions have consequences. I've been there and done that. But I've learned that what God wants from us all is our total dependence upon and complete TRUST in Him. He desires to reveal himself as our Loving Father in times of sadness, hardship, and pain. But we must trust Him by allowing Him to do so. Although I no longer have some of the materials and creature comforts I once had, what I do have every morning when I wake up is peace of mind.

My friend, remember this, **PEACE OF MIND is a priceless commodity that money cannot buy!**

Chapter 11

HEALING FROM THE PAIN

When you've experienced pain in life, it's imperative to give yourself time for healing before attempting to move forward. After going through some hardships and pain in my own life, I tried to be strong by masking my pain. There were many times I smiled while hurting deeply inside. You see my friend, sometimes the biggest smiles are covering the deepest pain. I tried staying busy and changing my focus by brushing my pain under a rug, but that only led to more pain to overcome. It was at my breaking point when I learned the valuable lesson that true proper healing MUST NOT be bypassed or shunned. I realized there was no way to heal unless I walked through the hurt. I also recognized that going through the pain does not mean pretending to be ok when you're not. You see, I needed to face the fact that it was no longer enough to act like I was ok, but I desperately needed to be ok from the inside. My heart needed healing. My mind needed healing. My spirit needed healing. There are times in life when we get lost on our journeys. The trials we go through can cause us to become cloudy. Our fragile minds and hearts can be negatively affected by circumstances, hardships, and pain. We find ourselves looking around trying to make sense of where we are in life. In trying to stay afloat and deal with life's circumstances we are sometimes thrown off our square. This is what happened to me.

Protecting my children was a priority for me. During my marital breakdown, no matter how much I was suffering, staying strong for my children during that time was my main focus. I can recall being so hurt and broken in my marriage and needing to release tears but held them in instead. There were many times I found myself using times of what should have been praise and worshiping God only for times of releasing tears of pain as well. In my mind I thought, "I can't allow my children to see me cry". I needed to be strong for them. But no matter how strong I tried to be, there were times when the tears would begin to flow without warning. Many Sundays I would drive to church with my daughter in the backseat and find myself weeping profusely and trying to dry my tears before pulling into the parking lot. After years of adorning myself with the "I'm ok mask" it became normal for me. I found myself acting tough when really, I wasn't. And I found myself acting unbothered when honestly, I was very bothered. You see I had also endured times, after the hurtful truth had been revealed in my marriage, when I would cry uncontrollably at home. But after being accused of using those tears as a weapon to hurt him, I took on the pressure of sparing his feelings by holding my tears. This was my way of easing his pain and keeping peace when what I really wanted and needed to do was scream, beat the floor and cry. I was made to feel guilty for feeling my pain. Imagine if you will, being deeply hurt by someone, then being told by that person that your response to the pain they've caused you makes them feel bad. Can you imagine that? This my friend is my truth. As feisty as I can be at times, I can't for the life of me understand why I allowed how he felt to dictate my actions, but I did. My mind had been manipulated so much during the end of my marriage I didn't quite know which way was up. So, what did I do? To appease him, I did my best to suppress my tears. By doing that, I was placing the desires and needs of others above my own needs. In a strange way I had taken on the responsibility of making him feel better after he had harmed me. Along with this, my children were my responsibility and staying strong for them during my marital trauma and through my divorce process was my top priority. I had gone into survival mode. I never stopped, I just kept going. While attempting to adjust I became ill. Amid regrouping, I became my dear mother's caregiver. Shortly thereafter, I lost both my mother and then two years later lost my father. It was somewhere during that time when I began approaching burnout and slowly losing my way. In doing so I came to some areas in my life that needed attention. God revealed to me places where I hadn't healed. I realized I hadn't grieved properly, I just kept going. Some of those places had turned into depression. Some of those places had turned into major difficulties with trust. Some of those places had turned into triggers. Since becoming aware I've made it a point to continue working on these areas in my life.

You see my friend, healing properly from your pain is very important. Healing properly doesn't mean masking or ignoring your pain as though you're strong enough to handle it alone. You may have some experiences in life that may cause you to go into survival mode. But remember, having the need to go into survival mode doesn't negate the importance of proper healing. Proper healing only takes place when you allow yourself to feel whatever you may feel and then allow God to heal those broken places in your heart. Remember there are no time limits on your healing process. Take it one day at a time my friend. Don't rush your healing process, allow yourself to go through it. Take baby steps and be patient with yourself. Don't try to paint it as anything other than what it is. God never pressures us on how long it should take us to heal. Therefore, my friend, please don't pressure yourself nor allow yourself to be pressured by anyone else. Simply allow yourself that valuable time of healing. Some paint on false faces and pretend to be strong, but somewhere along the way your true feelings and pain will resurface. Therefore, remember, no matter how long your healing process takes, healing from your pain is critical when trying to move forward.

Another thing to remember is that going into survival mode for others, but forgetting about yourself is also not the answer. There may be someone reading who understands how putting your needs on the back burner can easily become the norm. There is nothing wrong with taking care of your responsibilities whether it be, child, parent, or spouse. There's nothing wrong with being kind to others. The danger comes when taking care of others becomes more important than taking care of yourself. I totally understand you may be doing what you feel is natural as a spouse or parent or even a child. I realize there may be some like me who've had the experience of being a caregiver to a parent or loved one. And I understand how this responsibility may give you even more reason to put your needs on hold. There is nothing wrong with being a caring spouse, parent, or child. The danger comes in when taking care of yourself becomes LESS important than taking care of others. You are important my friend. By no means am I implying that others in your life aren't important, I am however, stressing the fact that YOU should be as important to you as others are to you. You should be as nice and kind to yourself as you are to others. After reaching an emotional overload, I realized that I deserved just as much of my own attention as I was willing to give others. I also realized that "I" matter to me. Today I feel absolutely no guilt in focusing on me. And when I talk about being focused on me, that doesn't mean focusing on me while forgetting about others, but I am yet learning to focus on myself as much as I do others. In fact, after God, I'm learning to love myself FIRST remembering that I am important!

Remember my friend, just as we are instructed on an airplane to put our masks on before helping someone else, the same applies in life. Don't allow taking care of others to become more important than taking care of YOU. We are commanded to love our neighbors **AS** we do ourselves. With that said, I ask you how can we love others correctly if we don't first love ourselves correctly? I urge you my friend to take the necessary time to love yourself. And don't be afraid of allowing your healing time to take place. Just as pain changes your life forever, the same goes for healing. Keep in mind that healing is for your own good. Your healing time could involve receiving therapy and if so that's ok. Please don't be too prideful to HEAL my friend. Your healing could involve taking a necessary break from a job, project, school etc. If so, my prayer for you is that you are not too stubborn to HEAL. Take that break or receive that therapy if needed to heal. Heal now in order to live later. Proper healing leads to wholeness and wholeness leads to the ability to begin loving yourself and fulfilling God's awesome purpose for your life!

Chapter 12

LOVE "YOU" AFTER THE PAIN

I'm not perfect. In fact, I consider myself to be perfectly imperfect. I realize that at times I have been what you would call "my own worst critic." But with all of the trials, flaws, and mistakes along my journey, I've learned and am yet learning to LOVE ME again. This hasn't been an easy process, but it gets better each day with God's daily grace, mercy, and unconditional love. One day as I reflected on my painful experiences and mistakes along my journey, I began beating myself up simply because my life wasn't where I wanted it to be. Have you ever had moments where you've reflected on things you wished you could undo or redo? At that moment God reminded me that I'm His child. He went on to remind me that He doesn't condemn me for my mistakes and that He was not happy with my self-condemnation. He then reminded me of my good attributes that uniquely make me who I am. He also reminded me of the fact that He knew every mistake I would make on my journey and STILL loved me enough to create me! He then refreshed my memory of how He had already forgiven me and took all my sin's past, present and future and paid for them all on the cross in my place! After He gently corrected me, He gave me strength to rise out of the depression. I realized that beating myself up for past mistakes, bad decisions, wrong moves is not the answer. Instead, I've learned to love who I am, embrace my pain, trials and mistakes, then allow them to continue making me a better and wiser person. Hating my mistakes is not an option! I realize that my mistakes have helped me become a BETTER me and for that I'm grateful! I encourage you to do the same my friend. Satan will try and use your mistakes to hold you mentally and emotionally hostage. But I say to you, "DON'T ALLOW IT"! If your past mistakes have been a source of pain for you, remember there is PURPOSE even in THAT pain. Recognize that you are not the mistakes you've made, but rather, what the mistakes have created! I see where my mistakes have made me a stronger woman! My mistakes have made me a wiser woman! My mistakes have helped me become more patient. My mistakes have taught me to trust and follow God's lead in every decision I make.

Sis, you are NOT your mistakes therefore, I encourage you to hold your head up! Don't continuously condemn yourself, but instead learn from your mistakes. Pick up your smile and start loving yourself again. We must remember we are human and as humans we will all make mistakes. The enemy comes to kill, steal, and destroy. His aim is to keep us mentally bound by past mistakes, but we must continue to remind ourselves that we are fearfully and wonderfully made! My brother, perhaps you've made some bad decisions in life. Have you been beat down mentally and emotionally because of those bad decisions? My encouragement to you is to lift your head and keep pressing forward! Don't allow your mistakes to define who you are! God doesn't beat us down, He's in the business of building us up! Remember, we won't always get it right, but no matter what you've done or how many times you've done it, God is the God of another chance! Therefore, no more holding your head down in shame and defeat! I encourage you to show the necessary remorse, repentance, and learn the necessary lessons. Continue walking tall in humility with the assurance and confidence of knowing who you are in Christ and that God is on your side! And for that reason, you have hope and a great future ahead! Yes, my friend we will all have to face adversity of all kinds. We will all slip and fall along the way. We will all suffer pain in this life. The God we serve is a gentleman and does not force Himself on us. But He instead gives us choices and it's up to us whether or not we want Him to be a part of our lives.

Although we will all suffer pain and face adversity, the wonderful thing is that with God's help, we don't have to face or endure the pain alone! I encourage you to allow God to help you through your painful season!

Your present situation may not be pleasant, but be encouraged knowing that God can and will work all your situations, circumstances, mistakes, pain and struggle out for your good! Remember our trials only come to make us strong! The only thing we are required to do is TRUST HIM. Hang in there my sister and don't give up my brother! What you're going through is only a test of your faith. Remember, seasons do change. Your troubles are not permanent! They are only steppingstones to something greater! There may be someone reading who is struggling from the painful memories of being molested. Believe it or not, God can even cause something good to come from that painful situation! Stay strong my friend, remembering that God has a purpose for every trial and test! I'm a firm believer that there is nothing too hard for God. Your suffering is not in vain. Expect something GOOD to come from it! We may not see the purpose, but rest assured that there is a purpose. God can cause something good to come from any painful situation.

I'm not taking for granted that everyone reading has a relationship with God. I won't force you, but I am inviting you to accept Him into your life. My friend, although it is true that we will all suffer pain in this life,

going through it with God's help is so much better than suffering alone with no relief. Every storm we encounter in life has the potential to destroy us, but the God of peace promises to guard our hearts and minds. As we courageously walk through the storms hand in hand with God, we will only lose those things that prevent us from being who God has called us to be such as sin, negativity, selfishness, and pride. Experiencing struggles, hardships, and pain gives us the opportunity to become more like Christ. After accepting Him as Lord of our lives, we must recognize that we are then extensions of Him. Our lives are no longer our own which means we don't have to face adversity alone. God never promises us a problem-free life here on earth, but He DOES promise to help us through our issues. No matter the hardship, mistakes, or pain, with God's help we will make it to the other side of the pain. My friend, you can try, but understand that you cannot make it to the other side of your pain by doing it alone. My encouragement to you is that you would lean into His strength by letting go of your issues and allowing God to help you through your issues.

He desires us to follow Him because He knows in doing so, we become more like Him.

How does this happen? It's all laid out for us in Mark 8:34 where it says, "Whoever wants to be my disciple must deny themselves and take up their cross and follow me." We live in a time where there Is so much focus on self. There are self-help books, podcasts, etc. So much emphasis on self-care and loving self. A phrase that has become popular is the phrase, "I'm doing me." Or we encourage others by saying, "Do you.!" And all of this is fine.

I'm a firm believer in the importance of loving yourself and following your dreams. I'm learning how to get better at this myself. But isn't it something that when giving guidelines to following Him the first guideline is to "deny self?" Denying yourself isn't easy, especially living in a "do you "world. But to truly follow Christ and do things His way we must first deny ourselves. My friend, my advice to you is that you'd not even attempt to "Do you" without first denying you and following Him. To deny yourself does NOT mean to hate yourself. The enemy wants us to think that denying self means to be miserable. He wants to twist our thinking about denying self into believing the lie that we must lose everything we love. Hearing "deny yourself" causes fear that we will somehow lose ourselves, however, denying yourself does NOT mean to hate yourself. It does NOT mean to lose yourself. To deny yourself means to daily get rid of the things that don't reflect Christ. As you deny yourself you'll begin loving all the beautiful and wonderful things that exist within you. Those unique things in you that make you who we are.

As I began denying myself my eyes were opened. It was then when I started seeing myself as God sees me. And the more I see myself as God sees me, the more I'm able to love myself. My friend, to deny yourself is the BEST way to Love yourself. When we deny ourselves by changing our negative thinking and ways, we begin taking on His thinking, and His ways. Denying ourselves for His sake is when we find ourselves. Remember, as we deny ourselves and choose to follow Him, He opens our eyes more to see as He sees. As we continue to get rid of the things that aren't like him during the pruning process, we begin reflecting Him more. You may not see an immediate change, but as you continue getting rid of those characteristics that aren't like Christ, you'll continue noticing changes from within. As you encounter situations that would normally make you angry, steal your peace or joy, you'll find yourself responding a different way. This my friend is called growth! When this happens, you're becoming more like Christ! We are not alone! There are many promises in His word to affirm and reaffirm that God is with us in our storms. Not only is He with us, but He is also making some good changes in us as we go through our storms!!

He will give us the strength we need to endure and persevere through every test and trial we may face. Maybe this is only me, but there have been times I didn't know how to love myself. My pain has sometimes caused me to focus on all the terrible things that have occurred in my life. There have been times when I allowed the setbacks in life cause me to not like myself. But I've learned to love myself! Today, I even like myself! I love my journey. It all makes me the woman I am today. I love the real parts of me that make me unique. There was a time when I didn't like having such a soft heart. But today I love my soft heart because it makes me compassionate towards others. And I also love that my eyes are open enough to see and accept the things in me that I still need to work on. Do you struggle with loving yourself? I understand my friend. God will show you how to love yourself despite your pain, mistakes, or setbacks. As you continue to inhale God's ways, God's wisdom, and unconditional love amid your tests and trials, you will be able to endure those tests and trials with joy believing by faith that He has a purpose for it all!

So, remember this my friend; **To Deny yourself is to Love yourself, and to Love yourself is to Deny yourself**. Continue getting rid of those negative characteristics that aren't Christ like. Then keep loving yourself no matter what. Loving yourself is not only enjoying a day at the spa. Love yourself by taking care of your health, taking care of your mind and most of all taking care of your spirit, by staying connected to the creator. When you do this my friend, you're loving yourself. In going through trials, we can sometimes lose ourselves and forget who God created us to be. There may be days when you struggle getting out of bed, combing your hair, responding to a text or call, and that's ok. But don't stay in that space. Don't give up. Don't get stuck in the pain. Don't get comfortable in self-condemnation! Pull yourself up and love "You" enough to fight for YOU! Encourage yourself! Remember you are God's beloved! Your enemy wants to keep you discouraged and focused on things that don't matter, but remember even in those times, God is in control. And remember, those things are only temporary!

No matter what your struggles, hardships or circumstances may be, you are amazing my friend, and God has an amazing future in store for you!

Chapter 13

AFTER THE PAIN

1 Peter 5:10 (NIV) states; "And the God of all grace, who called you to His eternal glory in Christ, after you have suffered a little while, will Himself restore you and make you strong, firm and steadfast."

This scripture is encouragement to us all. It echoes the fact that God is with us and no matter how much we suffer or how strenuous the troubles, or hardships may be, He promises to restore, He promises to make us strong, He promises to make us firm, and He promises to make us steadfast!

My friend, I thought about something one day. Sometimes in life we have the audacity to get upset with God during times of pain and suffering, but what we're really doing without realizing it is acting out of pride, as if to say, "I shouldn't be suffering like this." One day as I cried out to God, I had to ask myself the question, "Who are you to feel as though you shouldn't suffer or have difficulties in life?" After all Jesus suffered and He's the one I'm aiming to mirror. Therefore, I realized that if my goal is to become more like Him, then I must be willing to suffer and trust that He will help me through times of difficulty. You see, through each painful situation, through every trial and test, I've learned not to despise the journey, but instead embrace and thank God for it. Remember, it's the way you that you process and respond to pain that determines your outcome. No, it hasn't been easy, but I see how these experiences and more have strengthened my relationship with God. I no longer wonder IF He is going to be there for me during rough times, I ask Him for strength to endure the turbulence as He carries me through the storm! I know without any doubt that God is with me through every situation. And I trust that when facing times of adversity, God has a purpose for allowing it. Therefore, no matter how long it takes, I may cry from the heaviness of the pressure, but I NEVER lose faith in God's power and His word. So my friend, no matter how long "A little while" may take in your life, I urge you to trust Him through the process. What God wants from his children is our trust. He desires for us to lean completely on Him. No disrespect to our family and friends, but the truth is Man (humans) will fail you, but God NEVER fails! He wants our total dependence to be on Him! He wants us not only to talk to Him, but also LISTEN to Him and follow His guidance. He wants us to recognize that HE is our best friend and is in total control of our lives.

Remember that no matter what you have done in life, God still loves you unconditionally. In fact, He'll always love you unconditionally. Not only that, but He also has good plans for your life. When it feels like He's not with you, don't trust the feeling, but instead, trust His plan! No matter what negative situations you may face in life, God is with you. Remember He is there to help you and He will cause it all to work out for your good! There have been times in my life when I've wondered if God was still there. I have had time of wondering if He still had a purpose for my life. Pain and suffering have a way of bringing up wonder and doubt in your mind. But God assured me that my life mattered to Him. He has proven to be in total control of my life by carrying me through some horrific circumstances. Pain and suffering also have a way of causing you to fade into the background as it did me. After I had suffered "a little while" in the public eye, I began making myself comfortable in the background. I didn't want to be called to the front. I only wanted to heal. However, God reminded me during those times that He has a purpose for my life and choosing to be comfortable in the background did not change His plans for my life. Although I had been singing and encouraging others about Him for years, He allowed some things to happen in my life so that I could know Him personally in some areas. He allowed the tough times so that I would know Him a little deeper as my provider. Since being diagnosed with a potentially debilitating health condition, I now know Him personally as my healer! Since the deaths of my marriage and parents, God has been with me to comfort and supply everything I need. Now I realize that the only way to truly get to know who God is to experience His love, peace, comfort, protection, and provision personally during challenging times. Although none of my painful experiences felt good at the time, they were good for me and I'm grateful for each experience.

My friend, I pray that my story encourages you and helps you realize that you are not walking your journey alone. I pray that you are encouraged to include God in all of your decisions. I pray you're encouraged to know that your mistakes in life are not a death sentence. I encourage you to never forget that God loves you and has a purpose for all the pain you have suffered. If you have ever been mistreated, disrespected, humiliated, violated, verbally, mentally, or emotionally abused, remember God is with you to comfort your heart and He will cause something good to come from those painful experiences. Also remember that God never intended for His children to live in misery. He will give you strength to endure an unhealthy relationship. And He will make a way for you to exit a toxic relationship if needed. And if you trust Him enough, He will even replace those unhealthy relationships with healthy relationships. Our God is a loving Father. He will give you the wisdom needed to make the best decisions for your life. Trust that He will lead you to the decision that will ultimately give Him glory! Remember, God uses our storms to teach us that we need Him every second, minute and hour of everyday. He is our companion as we go through the valley of the shadow of death. The reason His word says that we do not have to fear evil is because He is with us! Keep in mind that our greatest testimony comes from our greatest pain! God uses our pain not to set us back, but to fuel us forward and direct our paths! All we simply need to do is to trust in God. Not only will He direct our paths, but He will also strengthen us to keep going. No matter how painful your journey may be, remember God is with you.

So don't fret when facing trials my friend. Keep in mind, His word says that after you have suffered a little while; He Himself will restore you, He will make you perfect and He will make you strong! He will support you and He'll place you on a firm foundation! No matter how long it takes or how far away He seems, God has not forgotten you! Jesus himself had to endure the pain of the cross, but remember the PURPOSE. He died so that we might live! But keep in mind, He would not have gotten to the resurrection without first going through the crucifixion (the pain). The point is, just as there was Purpose in His Pain, there is also Purpose in our Pain!

Chapter 14

BENEFITS OF PAIN

There may be someone reading who is thinking that there is no way that pain can be beneficial. Well, my friend, I beg to differ. Whether you believe it or not, pain is an important signal. Pain lets us know when something is wrong and needs extra care. Pain forces us to pay attention. Pain causes our focus to turn inward. Pain causes us to face those parts of ourselves that we might otherwise ignore.

Experiencing pain can prevent you from being injured further. Pain helps us appreciate pleasure. Pain gives us balance and reminds us of what is really important. Pain brings about positive change. Pain will one day allow you to comfort others with similar experiences. Pain will strengthen you. Pain brings clarity. The old saying "No Pain...No Gain" still stands true today. Pain unifies us because it is something that we will all experience. Experiencing pain brings about wisdom. Pain gives us a greater appreciation for the positives in our lives. Pain deepens our compassion and empathy towards others. Pain urges us to hold on a little tighter to those who are dear to your heart. Pain matures us to the point where we can admit, "I didn't always do things the right way." Pain helps us appreciate happiness and never take it for granted. My friend, pain helps us do better. Pain points us toward God! Pain leads us to trust in the Lord!

My friend, remember this, it is in our struggles where God is shaping us to be who He wants us to be. God is pruning us through our struggles which is a good thing. Yes, pruning is a painful process.

Although the pain can sometimes be excruciating, pruning also helps us. The pruning process enhances our spiritual growth by cutting away what is dead in our lives. That my friend is a GOOD thing! I don't know about you, but I want God to freely cut away anything that is dead in my life even if it hurts for "a little while"!

Jesus reminds us of who He is in John 15:1,2 (NIV) where He states, "I am the true vine, and my Father is the gardener. He cuts off every branch in me that bears no fruit, while every branch that does bear fruit, He prunes so that it will be even more fruitful" **There is a purpose in the pruning!** When pruning happens in our lives it allows room for new growth! Since God is the Gardener, He knows exactly what needs to stay in us and what we need to let go of. He desires His children to bear GOOD fruit! God allows suffering in our lives to strengthen our dependence on Him. It is our job as believers to trust Him during the pruning process. Continue to have faith that the pain you may experience from the pruning process will eventually benefit you!

> My friend, I understand how life does not always turn out the way we think it should.
>
> But keep in mind that, although experiencing pain may not feel good at the time, there are so many wonderful benefits to be gained from experiencing pain. You see my friend, with a different perspective, experiencing pain doesn't have to be something we dread. I am the first to admit that I have not always responded to my painful experiences in life the correct way. My aim in writing is NOT to appear blameless or as though I have it all together or have always done things the right way. On the contrary, there have been times in my own life when I allowed myself to fall into a "victim's mentality," which often led me to dread experiencing pain. I have sometimes fallen into the "poor

me" syndrome by feeling sorry for myself especially after being diagnosed with multiple sclerosis. I have experienced feeling as though I would never be happy again after the death of my marriage and the deaths of my parents. Over the years, after experiencing the pain of betrayal, I have struggled with trust issues. I did not like being guilty of having a "side eye" towards others, but because my trust had been broken, I did. And quite honestly at times, I still do. I call it ISP "Intense Self-Protection." I am only keeping it real my friend (don't judge me). Some experiences bring about wisdom and that is a good thing! I learned that I did not have to allow my distrust to become paranoia. Although I don't live my life paranoid, I do however watch everything, as well as pray because God's word instructs me to do so. Remember, protecting your heart and peace at all cost is also a form of loving yourself.

The problem comes when your self-protection turns into paranoia, or when painful experiences lead to negative emotions such as self-pity, worry, anxiety, fear, and doubt. We are human and will feel what humans feel. Nevertheless, we must focus on the fact that we do not have to feel those feelings with a victim's mentality. God helped me realize that I needed to reflect more on His word which tells me I am MORE than a conqueror! No, not on my own, but through Christ Jesus! I realized that although I have become more intentional about who I allow in my personal space, I do it not out of paranoia, but instead by using my God-given wisdom and discernment. When we go through painful experiences in life, remember He promises to strengthen our faith and endurance to keep going! For those who believe in God, our journeys are certainly faith walks. It's a faith walk because there will be times in life when we won't be able to see the forest for the trees. But it's during those times when we must dig deep inside, trusting that God has a plan, a purpose and our future in His hands. I encourage you once again to embrace the pain in your life with a different perspective. Prepare your heart to expect storms and difficulties so that you are not caught off guard when they come. But realize that the act of going through the pain is not the end for you. Continue moving ahead my friend. You might acquire some cuts and bruises along the way, but if you keep moving those cuts, bruises and deep wounds will turn into VICTORY scars! Remember scars are just reminders of what you have ALREADY come through with God's help!

So look forward to what going through the pain will produce in you! Remember not to disturb what God may be doing through the painful process. That is where the rejoicing comes in. You can rejoice because you know something GOOD is coming from the pain! What I am simply trying to convey is to trust God with your situations, circumstances, and pain. My friend, trusting in the Lord is very important throughout your journey. Without trust in Him. there can be no belief that He has a purpose in your pain. A lack of trust in God will lead to feelings of hopelessness. A lack of trust will lead to you taking matters into your own hands. A lack of trust in the Lord removes inner peace. A lack of trust in the Lord promotes the very false notion that you are in total control of your life when honestly, that's the furthest thing from the truth.

Yes, life can sometimes be difficult, but you do not have to manage life alone. God is there to help you in any situation. Let it go, allow Him to carry you through your process then watch everything work out for your good! God has brought me through some life-changing events and as a result I am not the same Freshun. I have been changed for the better! There are things about Freshun that are new and improved! Through my pain He pointed out some things I needed to be aware of. Through my pain He highlighted areas in which I needed more dependence upon Him. No, it did not feel good at the time, but

God used my pain as a teaching tool. He allowed me to endure painful situations along the way that only He and I are aware of. Since getting through the pain in my life, I am happy to share with you today that it didn't kill me! Instead, today I'm a stronger Freshun! To God Be ALL the Glory!

CONCLUSION

Thank you, my friend, for taking the time to read my story. I pray that in reading, you have found some nuggets along the way that will encourage and strengthen you as you walk out your personal journey. When you face trials in life my prayer is that you will remember that you are not alone. If I did not mention your specific source of pain, the main point I would like you to remember is to be courageous and TRUST that God is with you no matter what your source of pain or struggle may be!

I thought that having Multiple Sclerosis would be more than I could ever manage, but God has kept me and proven that He is in total control of my health! When my heart had been overtaken with grief after the loss of my parents, and depression tried to set up residence in my heart, God soothed my aching heart! When my finances took a major hit, God supplied and continues to supply all my needs! Times when I felt too weak to keep going, God became my strength! Therefore, I make the choice to trust Him no matter what comes. His word says that He has overcome the world which includes everything! Therefore, we can trust that no matter what our setbacks may be, He will use what we see as setbacks as setups for our comebacks! Do you remember Job in the Bible? He lost everything! But even after losing everything, his response was, ***"Though he slay me, yet will I trust in him" (Job 13:15 KJ***V). In the end, God gave him double for his trouble! This is the type of trust we must have. Continue trusting God through your trials just as Job did. Remember that with every setback comes maturity and completion! So, don't worry about your setbacks. God has our best interest at heart and will cause something good to come from our pain and setbacks! I don't have the answer as to how He does it, but I do know that He can and will. He tells us in His word to be strong and courageous because He knows we will face circumstances that may cause us to shy away and become fearful or dreadful. But remember to focus NOT on the pain itself, but rather on the outcome of what going through the pain can produce! Focus on the fact that you are going to be BETTER after the pain! Remember that your season of suffering is only temporary! Your trouble will only last a little while, and after a little while God Himself will Restore you! After a little while, He will strengthen you! And after a little while, He will establish you! One definition of the word "establish" found in Webster's dictionary is "to put in a position or role that will last a long time!" In oxford languages, the word establish means to set up! In being a part of the acting industry, I've noticed how it's everyone's desire to get that "featured or recurring role " in a film. I don't know about you, but I want the Lord to set me up by placing me in a role that will last a long time! Having connections or hookups in life is all right, but I'd rather GOD set me up than man! When God sets you up, you are only indebted to Him! I encourage you to walk with God through your pain and allow Him to turn your pain and setbacks into setups for your amazing comeback!

I've learned that the paths I chose to travel may have delayed some things in my life, but nothing has been canceled. Therefore, I'm thankful for my journey and excited about what is to come! I have learned that although we will endure some pain and hardships on our journeys, it does not have to control the narrative of our lives. God continues to prove that I, Freshun Eleana Wilson, am important to Him. Please do not get me wrong, I am not saying that my life is perfect, that would be a lie. However, I am saying that with every challenge God has been there guiding me, teaching me, keeping me, and providing for me through them all.

When my finances have gotten low, I have learned during those tough times how to be content in whatever state I find myself in. When the enemy tried to convince me that I would never have anything and never be happy again, God has proven those words to be wrong by continuing daily to supply my every need! Although my heart was devastated and overcome with fear when finding out I had Multiple Sclerosis, I now have peace about my condition knowing God is my healer. Today, I can bathe and dress myself, hold a pen, and sign my own name! I give all glory to God for the activities of my limbs because there have been days when I could not do those things. Therefore, my friend, I have learned to take nothing for granted. I now personally know God as my healer and for this, I am eternally grateful!

I have been what some call a "church girl" all my life. I've believed what I've been taught over the years, but when you experience His keeping power personally, it "hits a little different" as they say. The trials I have endured in life have all strengthened my trust and faith in God's power. My father taught me to sing hymns and Gospel music before I had any idea of what all the words truly meant. But it is because of the tests and trials God has brought me through that I am now able to sing with an even deeper conviction than before. It's been through the tests and trials of life that I've experienced the encouraging truths of those songs. I know without one doubt who holds my tomorrow. My faith in Him is much stronger. Having lost some who, I thought were friends along the way, God has proven himself to be my absolute best friend. I trust Him with my entire life. Although I have not always done what was right, God has never let me down. He has never hurt my feelings. What He has done is proven to me in so many ways that He is on my side, and He is with me.

My friend, I can't reiterate enough that no matter how rough the pain and struggles may be in your life you are not alone. God is with you and God will work every trial out for your GOOD! I'm a living witness to this my friend. **You see, my PAIN led to my journaling. My journaling through the pain led to the book you are reading today!** If you need more proof, please allow me to be your living proof! This is an example of how God will cause something good to come from your pain! Although I did not fully understand all details of the assignment, I trusted God, obeyed, and kept writing! This taught me to never limit myself and never limit God!

There was a time when I thought that my purpose in life would only be connected to music somehow. And while that is partially true, little did I know that through my pain God would develop in me another gift through which His goodness can be shared with others. **My first book has been born out of journaling through my pain!** Before journaling, I had never considered writing as one of my gifts or talents. In my mind, I was simply writing through my pain, but I am so thankful that God continued to instruct me to "Keep writing." And although the enemy attempted to stop me, I am even more thankful that I listened and obeyed His instructions! This is an example of God's ways not being our ways and His thoughts not being our thoughts. Becoming an author was not a childhood dream or passion for me, but it was in GOD'S plan! Not only am I able to use my voice as a musical instrument for God's glory, but He has also birthed in me a different method through which I can share His goodness with others. Although the enemy TRIED to silence my voice through acts of malicious behavior, glory to God it didn't work! What the enemy means for evil in our lives, God will use it for good!

My friend if you recall, I started out by letting you know that none of what you are reading is fictional. I chose to share some experiences from my own life for the sole purpose of first glorifying God and then to encourage others. If God can bring me through all my storms, which He did, He will do the same for you! Trust Him through your pain sis! God is there with you. Don't crumble under the pressures of life my brother! Hang in there believing by faith that there is nothing is too hard for God! He will instruct you on how to manage all of the details in your life. My advice to you is to Seek His wisdom on what He may want you to learn through your circumstances.

Don't fight it or ignore it. But go through it and allow the pain to do what it needs to do in you. Allow the pain to reveal what needs to be revealed. Allow the pain to teach you. Allow the pain to make the necessary changes in you for the better. While going through the pain, keep anticipating all the good that is being produced through the pain!

Keep believing by faith and declaring to yourself that "something good is going to come from this!"

Sometimes getting to the other side of pain involves taking steps. As in my case sometimes those steps may involve letting go of the familiar. Sometimes those steps may involve walking away from toxic comfort zones that have become hazardous to your health. Those steps are not always easy to make. Yes, my sister. I understand how those steps can be frightening. I made those steps with three young children and a lengthy career that consisted of taking care of my family with no pension or 401K. Yes, my friend, walking into the unknown can be overwhelmingly fearful, but keep trusting God every step of the way! You may not understand why but keep trusting Him. To every woman who has ever been told or made to feel that she can't make it, I encourage you to believe the very opposite and trust God! God loves you. He loves you not because of any earthly attachment, but He loves you because you are His. God is aware of all you have been through, and He has His own sweet way of rebuilding your God-confidence and confirming just how precious you are to Him. This is something He has done for me. Although your situation may appear hopeless, keep trusting Him. You may be too mentally drained to press forward, but use the little strength you do have and continue pressing forward! I encourage you to make YOU a priority. Gods got you! Through your fear trust God! Through your pain and confusion trust God and lean into His wisdom and strength to carry you! I understand how no one desires to go through the pain of divorce, especially with children. It's not an easy thing to do. But, if you must walk away from a dying/toxic relationship that's no longer glorifying God, walk away trusting God with all the consequences. I'm a witness that He will guide you through the process. It's not the end of the world. However, it could very well be if you choose to stay in a toxic environment. It could also be the beginning of living a peaceful life. No, I am not speaking as an advocate for divorce. Nevertheless, I am speaking as an advocate for living a peaceful, joyful, and abundant life! No, not a perfect or trouble-free life, but a life of mental peace and emotional freedom. Just to recap, yes, trouble will come, but don't forget God is with you and will carry you through the trouble. Remember that living a life of misery is NOT one of God's promises to us. He never instructed us to sacrifice our lives. Instead, HE came to give us LIFE more abundantly! You see my friend, God's purpose for creating us was not for us to die in our pain, but instead to live beyond our pain with Him! To anyone that needs to hear this, DYING IN YOUR MARRIAGE IS NOT GOD'S WILL FOR YOUR LIFE! Trust Him to lead you and to make your path clear my friend, and I'm certain He will. Now that I'm on the other side of the pain I'm glad I didn't give up. I now realize that I was created to outlive marital struggles and a horrific divorce! I was created to live through carrying a potentially debilitating condition! God did not allow those things to happen for the purpose of killing me. I trust and believe that His plans are to prosper me and not harm me! His plans are to give hope and a future!

Through fear and uncertainty, believing God's word gave me the courage to walk away from a painful situation towards my hope and my future! His plans for you are the same. Always remember, it was not God's plan for the pain you experience in life to kill you, therefore do not allow your pain to kill you by remaining in a toxic relationship. Yes, my friend, **"pain is a reality, but it is NOT a fatality!"** With God's help we were born to conquer our pain and move forward in life with Him! Remember not only are we conquerors, but with Christ we are MORE than conquerors! Trust Him to lead you in the direction that is best for you. Trust Him to carry you through every circumstance of your life. My friend, although my journey has not been perfect, it has been perfect for ME! I have learned and grown through my struggles, mistakes, and painful experiences. Today I am appreciative of every struggle and for my growth. God has proven to be with me through every trying circumstance. Through marital struggles and divorce, through the pain of betrayal, through shame and humiliation, through times of feeling unappreciated, through mental and emotional abuse, through a devastating diagnosis, through the loss of my mother and father, through major financial difficulty, through times I had lost myself and times of depression, through major complications from my health condition, I know without a doubt that God has been and remains with me and STILL has an awesome plan for my life! I have learned to take every step and season in stride, trusting God with ALL circumstances and believing by faith that somehow, He has the power and will work it everything out. The highs and lows, the good and bad, the joys and pains, He will work it all out for my good!

Because of the pain I have experienced, today I am closer and more dedicated to God. I am wiser. I am stronger. I am more disciplined. I am more courageous. My faith is stronger. I am tougher in some areas, and more tender and understanding in others, I am more forgiving, I'm unbothered by the insignificant. I am more patient. I am more empathetic and sympathetic towards others. I am more loving and more intentional! And through it all I have learned to love me! To wrap it up concisely, I am so much BETTER than I was before!

Remember, when you encounter pain, adversity or trauma in life, it is human to feel it. Whether we admit it or not, we all feel pain. Pretending we are supernatural does not make the pain go away. So then why make it a habit of painting on fake smiles to hide deep pain? My friend I urge you to instead allow God to heal your heart and help you through the pain! Keep allowing yourself to feel whatever you need to feel. Attempts to numb the pain only prolongs the pain and delays the healing.

Allow yourself the much needed sufficient time of healing, otherwise you will find the pain continuing to surface at other times and in other areas of your life. To those who are grieving a devastating loss of a loved one, it is my personal belief that there is not a professional on this earth who can accurately advise you on how long your grieving process should last. But I will simply say from my experiences that if you keep trusting in God and leaning into His strength, no matter how long it takes, you will smile again. Don't focus on getting "over" it. Honestly my friend, that may never happen. But focus on getting "through" it. I know firsthand that God will give you the daily strength to continue living despite the holes that exist in your heart after losing a loved one.

One day He may even present an opportunity for you to be a blessing to someone else during their time of grief.

To you who may be feeling hopeless, yes, God DOES have a purpose for your life! The enemy sees your potential and desires to take you out. He wants to cancel out your destiny by causing you to cave under pressure, but be strong in the Lord my friend. God has something great in store for you and He has already worked any trial you may face out for your good! It is not our job to know how He will do it, but instead to simply trust that He'll do it!

Be encouraged! Whatever your circumstances may be, my prayer is that you will not allow your painful experiences or extreme hardships cause you to quit and forfeit God's wonderful plans for your life! My friend, you matter to God. Settling in your pain is not the answer, but instead taking those necessary steps to get THROUGH your pain. Those steps include trusting God no matter what. You see my friend; the enemy has a plan. Your enemy wants you to believe that you have no purpose for being alive. He wants you to believe that you're a failure. He wants you to believe that you would be better off remaining in a toxic situation. Your enemy wants you to live your life believing that you have no hope for a better tomorrow. The enemy will attempt to convince you that staying in misery for the convenience of having material "stuff" is best for you. However, remember that God's plans for you are so much better than choosing a life of misery. The enemy wants you to believe that your struggles are permanent, but always believe the very opposite of what he says! During my financial struggles, the enemy has never ceased to remind me of the materials I left behind when I chose to walk away from my marriage, but I laugh at the enemy! Because although I may not have some of the material things I once had, what I do have is peace of mind and I'd much rather have God's peace than anything money can buy.

Remember, whatever it is you may be going through, struggling with, or hurting from, it is all temporary! Your enemy wants you to believe that you cannot make it through this season in your life, but I am living proof that you can, and you will make it to the other side of your pain! My friend, remember our stories are for HIS GLORY!

My aim is to inspire and encourage all who are reading to keep praying, keep praising, keep worshiping, keep pressing, keep walking and keep trusting God through your trials! My friend, keep in mind that although storms in your life may cause you to bend, with God on your side you won't break beyond repair! No, it won't always be easy, but you will come through it, and you will be a better person because of it! Therefore, keep walking towards your "better day ", and as you do, you will see that your tomorrow is much better than yesterday. I understand how the trials of life can sometimes cause your faith to waiver, but remember, God has not allowed the pain in your life to harm you, but instead to test your faith in Him and to strengthen your dependence on Him. Most importantly, God has allowed your pain to mature and complete you! Can you see how the pain is working for your good? My friend, don't throw in the towel and give up when times get tough. I encourage you to keep allowing God to show Himself strong in your life! As you walk through your process, continue to trust him, keeping in mind that on the other side of your pain you will find Peace, Joy, Abundant Life and a purpose for it all! During your most challenging times, my prayer is that you will keep allowing perseverance to finish its perfect work in you. In other words, don't back down, and don't give up! Allow the pain to do what it needs to do in you! No matter what painful experiences you may have to endure in this life, remember God will cause them all to work out for your good! Therefore, don't be thrown by storms, trouble, pain, or adversity my friend.

Keep in mind that suffering is something we will all have to endure in this life, one way or another. BUT, the comforting thing for us all to remember is that, despite the severity of our past, present, or future circumstances, God is ALWAYS with us and there is still an AMAZING PURPOSE in the Pain that He allows in our lives!

ABOUT THE AUTHOR

Freshun E. Wilson is a native of East St. Louis Il. She is the proud mother of H. Levi IV, Christopher and Jazmyn. Freshun is an accomplished vocalist and has served faithfully for many years as lead vocalist and music director in different ministries across the Midwest in cities inclusive of East St. Louis Il., Decatur, Il., Chicago, Il., as well as Lansing MI.

After taking a leap of faith in moving to Atlanta Ga., Freshun has been afforded many opportunities in the acting and film industry including being featured with Mr. Greg Kirkland and TheSEEit Choir in the Tyler Perry Movie "A Madea Family Funeral" and the National Geographic Series Genius: Aretha, as well as starring with Mr. Tony Terry in the stage play "A love like this" The love story of Ruth and Boaz, and the stage play "Deliver me from self", just to name a few.

Presently many know her as a vocalist, music director, cosmetologist, and actress, but have no idea of her struggle into recapturing "Freshun" after experiencing and overcoming some very painful seasons in her life.

Finally, in her freshman book, "Purpose in the Pain", Freshun shares her personal journey in hopes that every reader would be inspired, empowered and encouraged to NEVER give up during times of pain and adversity!

Printed in the USA
CPSIA information can be obtained
at www.ICGtesting.com
LVHW012027201023
761657LV00080B/1664

9 781662 866357